IMPACT OF BANK INTEREST RATES ON SHG MEMBERS

About the Authors

Prof. D Rajasekhar, who heads the Centre for Decentralisation and Development at the Institute for Social and Economic Change, Bangalore, India, is a Development Economist. With vast experience in social science research, he has been providing policy support to the government, donors, NGOs, etc. He has undertaken many research studies for the government and external agencies such as the World Bank, ILO, GTZ, etc. He was the team leader for a major research study on *'Roles of Local Organisations in Development Projects'*, supported by the World Bank. He has published 12 books and over 40 research articles in various journals and edited books.

Mr. N Krishne Gowda is working at the Centre for Decentralisation and Development, Institute for Social and Economic Change, Bangalore. He has been specialising in the areas of micro-finance through self-help groups, and child labour.

Ms. R Manjula is working at the Centre for Decentralisation and Development, Institute for Social and Economic Change, Bangalore. Her areas of interest include micro-finance, fiscal decentralisation, and gender and collective action.

IMPACT OF BANK INTEREST RATES ON SHG MEMBERS

A Study in Grama Vikas Project Area

D Rajasekhar
N Krishne Gowda
R Manjula

Published for
Grama Vikas and NOVIB

by

CONCEPT PUBLISHING COMPANY, NEW DELHI-110059

Cataloging in Publication Data—DK
Courtesy: D.K. Agencies (P) Ltd. <docinfo@dkagencies.com>

Rajasekhar, D. (Durgam), 1960-
Impact of bank interest rates on SHG members : a study in Grama Vikas project area / D. Rajasekhar, N. Krishne Gowda, R. Manjula.
p. cm.
Study conducted in Kolar District, Karnataka, India.
Includes bibliographical references (p.)
Includes index.
ISBN 8180692930

1. Rural development projects—India—Kolar (District)—Finance. 2. Microfinance—India—Kolar (District). 3. Interest rates—India—Kolar (District). 4. Self-help groups—India—Kolar (District). I. Krishne Gowda, N., joint author. II. Manjula, R., joint author. III. Title.

DDC 332.095 487 22

ISBN 81–8069–293-0

First Published 2006

Published and Printed by
Ashok Kumar Mittal
Concept Publishing Company
A-15/16, Commercial Block, Mohan Garden
New Delhi (INDIA)

Phones : 25351460, 25351794
Fax : 091–11–25357103
Email : publishing@conceptpub.com

Foreword

NABARD started a programme in 1992 to link self-help groups (SHGs) formed for disadvantaged and poor women with the banks. This programme has been innovative in many ways. The choice of poverty-stricken rural women as the principal beneficiaries of the programme might have been considered as rather unwise, and even risky, by many when the programme was launched. It was hard to imagine that the rural women belonging to the lowest strata could be persuaded to save and create a financial base for the SHG activities. It would have appeared even more preposterous for many that these women were expected to deal with sophisticated institutions like banks and even undertake own account income generating activities. However, the record of SHGs has been remarkable. According to the latest fact sheet available on NABARD website, as on 31 March 2005, there were 1,618,456 SHGs with the women groups forming 90 per cent of them. Over 70 per cent of SHGs were formed by the NGOs. 24.25 million households were assisted up to this date. Average loan per assisted family was Rs. 3,044. Over forty thousand bank branches participated in the programme giving loans amounting to nearly Rs. 70 billion.

The evaluations show that the repayment performance of the members has generally been excellent leaving little reason for the banks to feel aggrieved. Going by the media reports, SHGs seem to be tainted with far fewer scams compared to mainstream institutions like banks and cooperative societies! There are, of course, areas where SHGs have not done well. Income generating activities (IGAs) have seriously lagged with the loans being used predominantly for non-productive/consumption purposes. The dependence of the members on moneylenders and other informal sources of credit has not been eliminated. In fact, it is likely that the commendable repayment performance of SHG members has been achieved at the cost of borrowing from informal sources. It is easy to criticise SHGs and their members and supporters for these weaknesses. Currently, the critics of SHGs and of microfinance seem to be more numerous and more vocal than those pleading the case of SHGs for continuing support and encouragement. It is important to set the record straight and view the SHG programme as a part of the ongoing process of empowerment of the poor. And empowerment of the poor, as we argue, cannot be assessed on the basis of economic criteria alone. This needs to be looked from several other dimensions though it is true that the ultimate viability and development thrust of programmes like SHG does depend on the fulfilment of economic criteria. At the present juncture of formative stage of SHGs, one should be careful not to overstress the economic criteria nor to lose sight of other indicators of progress of empowerment.

For this purpose, the emergence of SHGs, in our view, needs to be placed in the broader development context in India and the forces shaping it. Markets are notorious for bypassing the poor and the backward. In India, very ironically for a nation which reveres Mahatma Gandhi as its father, even the developmental policy regime as a whole has let down the poor with rural women being its worst and very tragic victims. Bias towards organised industries and capital-intensive technologies in our growth-promoting policies, low priority accorded to agriculture and inadequate investments in rural infrastructures and in conservation and development of land and water resources are among the prominent manifestations of the neglect of rural areas and of the poor in our development strategies and programmes. It was obvious by the early 90s that India was doing little to help the poor beyond the poorly implemented relief programmes. More important, there was growing recognition that the moves towards major economic reforms launched during this period needed to be complemented with programmes for empowerment of the poor and for enabling them to participate in local governance and development planning. The constitutional amendment enacted during this period to establish the Panchayati Raj Institutions (PRIs) as the third tier of government was a historic step in that direction. Simultaneously, there was a veritable boom in the activities of NGOs and civil society activists to sensitise the poor and to organise them for demanding their rights and basic needs.

The NABARD initiative to develop SHGs involved in

microfinance fitted well in this emerging situation as indicated by the spectacular growth in SHGs mentioned above. Institution building is a slow process. Members need time to develop mutual trust and understanding. Taking up own account activities in a globalising economy needs not only acquisition of production skills but, even more, finding markets for one's product and responding to changes in them while remaining ahead of competitors. Even producers in organised sectors clamour for help from the government to meet these challenges. SHGs are yet to cross this hurdle and there is a risk that their development would remain blocked at the stage of pooling the savings of members and modest borrowing from the banks to meet the day-to-day consumption needs and to tide over the episodes of sickness and family celebrations. This is still an achievement for the women belonging to the poorest strata but not a remedy to overcome their chronic poverty. When SHGs are considered in the context of the prevailing rural setting and the policy regime for agricultural and rural development, the constraints facing SHGs are seen to be too formidable to overcome with their own efforts alone.

This study by Professor Rajasekhar and his colleagues is very timely and valuable for the light it throws on these constraints. The twenty SHGs covered in the study are located in severely drought-prone parts of Kolar district in Karnataka. To add to the woes of the SHGs, this area suffered from drought for three successive years including the year (2003) in which the research team met the SHGs and their members. The important point to note is that drought-proofing through watershed development and adoption of dryland technologies is quite feasible in Karnataka if only the necessary policy initiatives are taken and implemented with a sense of commitment. This has not happened so far. The watershed projects in Karnataka have hardly had any impact excepting a few villages where there was good local leadership or active NGO. The point is that the beneficial impact of watershed could be observed within the state but the policy maker has shown little interest in implementing it on a scale large enough to cover the extensive drought-prone areas in the state. The bore-wells have been allowed to over-exploit the ground water so that those who depend on them suffer as much in drought as those not having irrigation. Thus, the heavy costs which the droughts impose on the poor in Karnataka are man-made rather than an act of unkind nature. This study brings out quite convincingly how even promising IGAs wither and are ultimately abandoned given the risks of losses imposed by droughts. Only exceptions like dairying survive in the households which manage well their access to irrigation because of dependable arrangements for marketing and processing. Many other activities have similar potential but do not receive the policy maker's attention which dairying receives. Thus, the prospects for IGAs remain dim for SHGs given the prevailing policy regime and its persistent biases and failures.

The other point which stands out in this study is the unhelpful attitude of the banks towards SHGs. A valuable exercise which Professor Rajasekhar and his team have done is to estimate the transaction costs involved in microfinance operations and the manner in which they are shared by the two parties to the transaction—banks and SHGs. Their exercise brings out quite well the heavy burden carried by the SHGs and the manner in which banks add to this burden instead of reducing it by suitably streamlining their own operations and procedures. As a result, the effective interest rate the SHGs pay was observed to be as high as 24 per cent, a rate which is inconceivable in the organised mainstream industries. It needs to be mentioned that the interest rate paid by the SHG members would be even higher as part of their borrowings are from costly and merciless informal sources of borrowings. Despite this situation heavily loaded against the members, their repayment performance has been and continues to be good. Ironically, the banker seems to benefit more from microfinance than the SHG members! While the latter barely manages to live a life of hard work and drudgery, the banker can look forward to promotions and comfortable city postings based on his good work to help the poor! This phenomenon should be of particular interest to social science researchers as it shows that when the elites and the poor interact—whether in labour market, produce market or poverty alleviation programmes—the initiative, bargaining power and the larger share of benefits accrue to the elite and the poor get too little to make any substantial improvement in their status or economic conditions. The poor are certainly better off with SHG than without. However, the direct and enduring benefits may turn out to be very modest.

There is a hopeful twist in the story told by this study. Armed with this study, the NGO helping the SHGs did some hard and persistent lobbying in Delhi and was rewarded by a 3.5 per cent reduction in the interest rate charged by the banker! The moral of the story is that the SHG members, besides practising the virtue of prompt repayment, should learn the skills capable of giving them a decent livelihood and organisational and lobbying clout to deal with the elites. The poor should imbibe the important lesson that their genuine and enduring empowerment would come not from the large-hearted kindness of the elite but from their own readiness and ability to confront the elite. Economic improvements are essential to the poor but they will be able to enjoy it only when they can pose a credible threat to the elite to wrest it from them if that becomes unavoidable. Professor Rajasekhar and his colleagues deserve to be commended for this perceptive study which has the unusual distinction of bringing some relief to the poor even before its publication! It is a happy thought that there are academics who are ready to shun the comforts of modern ivory towers—libraries and seminar halls—when this becomes necessary to get a first hand view of the field and its poor dwellers!

Bangalore **V M Rao**
October 2005

Preface and Acknowledgements

The Study on 'Impact of Bank Interest Rates on SHG Members' was undertaken by Prof. D. Rajasekhar, Mr. N. Krishne Gowda and Ms. R. Manjula. The main purpose behind undertaking this study was to find out whether there was any justification for initiating advocacy to reduce interest rates on bank loans through NABARD programme. In the process of completion of this study, a number of institutions and individuals provided very good help and support.

We acknowledge, with gratitude, the support, encouragement and co-operation provided by NOVIB, which has been supporting our endeavour to organise the poor women in Mulbagal taluk and empower them. When we suggested that this study would help us in our advocacy efforts, NOVIB readily agreed to provide the necessary financial support.

Prof. V.M. Rao, Visiting Professor, Institute for Social and Economic Change, Bangalore, has very kindly written the foreword to the book. This adds, I am sure, to the merit of this book. I thank him profusely for his kindness. I also thank Mr. V.S. Parthasarathy for his excellent support in carrying out the editorial changes in the manuscript.

Before the study was actually launched, an initial meeting was organised with the SHG members to discuss and seek their opinion about the interest rates on bank loans. The Executive Committee members of *Mahila Okkuta* also made very good points relating to the ways in which high bank interest rates were adversely affecting poor women. In particular, I would like to thank Mrs. Jayalakshmi, Treasurer and Mrs. M.G. Papamma, Secretary, *Mahila Okkuta.* I also thank my colleagues Ms. M.S. Girija, Ms. T.C. Pavithra and Mr. K.V. Ramesh for their help and co-operation during the entire process of undertaking this study.

I thank the Managers of Bank branches (Kolar Grameena Bank, Canara Bank, State Bank of Mysore, etc.) who spared their precious time with the study team in providing the required information.

I wish to place on record my sincere thanks to Ms. Kusuma, Ms. Bhavana and Ms. Gayathri for their enthusiastic help to the study team in data collection in all the 20 sample villages and in organising meetings with SHGs and banks.

The main actors in this study are members of the self-help groups. I cannot forget their contribution. They enthusiastically participated in the meetings held with the study team and spent their valuable time in sharing their experiences with the SHG linkage programme. These experiences strengthened our conviction that we should lobby against the bank interest rates.

M.V.N. Rao
Executive Director, Grama Vikas,
Honnsetthalli, Yelagondahalli PO
Mulbagal Taluk, Kolar District-563 127

Contents

List of Tables and Cases

Tables

Cases

1

Introduction

Grama Vikas is a NGO working with women belonging to depressed castes and economically vulnerable groups in Mulbagal taluk in Kolar district for the last two decades. The organisation has initiated a study on the 'impact of bank interest rates on SHG members' in its project area. This study aims to assist the Grama Vikas in its advocacy work relating to interest rates on bank loans through NABARD's bank-SHG linkage programme.

In 1992, NABARD initiated a programme to link SHGs formed by the NGOs and other organisations such as banks, for both poverty alleviation and to achieve cost-effectiveness in reaching a large number of small borrowers in the rural areas. The programme has made rapid progress in the last one decade in Karnataka, in particular, and India, in general.

Grama Vikas was one of the first organisations in Karnataka to realise the importance of linkage banking in its development programme, and initiated the linkage process in 1994 itself. Since then, the organisation has been striving to operationalise the bank-SHG linkage programme in its project area. Between 1994 and 2003, the organisation enabled its target group to obtain 2,736 loans, and the total loan amount involved was Rs.1.21 crores. Further, the Grama Vikas lobbied with NABARD for improvement in the programme components and implementation. Accordingly, it organised several consultation meetings with the officials from NABARD and banks in the project area to advocate the cause of SHG members and bring qualitative changes in the programme implementation.

Although the programme has made considerable progress in quantitative terms, a few concerns are often raised. In the context of a steep decline in the interest rates on bank deposits and different types of loans, several NGOs have expressed concern about the high interest rates on SHG loans at 12.5 per cent, emphasising the need for its reduction. Further, since the poorer sections covered under the programme earn their livelihood in adverse socio-economic and weather conditions, high interest loans result in smaller income from the activities assisted under the programme. This, in turn, leads to inability to invest in the activity and to incur expenditure on health, education and other subsistence needs.

Grama Vikas in its interactions with the people has found that the members were finding it difficult to obtain sufficient income to repay the loan with interest, reinvest into the activity and meet the social expenditure of the household. In its discussions with the people, the organisation has also learnt that the member borrowers repaid the loans by curtailing the expenditure on food, clothing, education and health. Further, some of the members had been forced to repay the loans by selling the productive assets that they had acquired through NABARD loan and/or through their own sources. In some other cases, the loan had to be repaid through borrowals from moneylenders at high interest rates. Grama Vikas is concerned that all these are coming in the way of achieving the programme objectives of asset building, income generation and poverty reduction.

It is in this context that a study to examine the effects and ramifications of bank interest rates on SHG members was undertaken. The main objectives of the study were to:

1. arrive at transaction costs incurred by the banks and SHGs under the programme of NABARD on Bank-SHG linkage;
2. analyse the impact of interest on income from the activity, investment into the activity and meeting the expenditure incurred on subsistence needs; and
3. find out whether there was any justification for advocacy to reduce interest rates on bank loans through NABARD programme.

Hypotheses

- The high interest rates on ultimate borrowers under the Bank-SHG linkage programme adversely affect reinvestment in the activity and the expenditure on food, health and education.

- Transaction costs incurred by the banks under the linkage programme are low and make a case for reduction in the interest rates.
- SHGs and their members incur high transaction costs in linkage programme and the interest income earned under the programme does not cover these transaction costs.

Instruments

This study has used structured questionnaires to elicit the following information from members and representatives of SHGs and bank officials.

- **Household questionnaire:** information on the socio-economic condition of the household, demographic profile and total amount of savings contributed in the sample group; information on loans that the households obtained in the last three years from different sources; and information on the activity for which the loan was utilised, income from the activity, reinvestment, and sources of repayment.
- **SHG questionnaire:** Data on how and when the linkage with the bank was established, costs incurred by the group to establish linkage with the banks, involvement of the group in the selection, monitoring and repayment of loans and the data on amount paid and repayment status.
- **Bank questionnaire:** Number of SHGs obtaining credit facility from the service area of the bank branch and total amount of assistance provided; the type of support services provided to SHGs by the banks; and perceptions of the bankers on the utility of the linkage programme to the bank branch.

Further, data on the perceptions of the members, SHG representatives and bankers on interest rates and whether there was any need to reduce the same were obtained in all the questionnaires.

Sampling Design and Size

Although 246 SHGs in the Grama Vikas project area obtained loan facility from the banks during 1994–2003, the groups obtaining bank loans during 2000 and 2001 were considered ideal for the purpose of drawing sample for the following reasons:

- If groups obtaining loans before 1999 were selected, the process adopted in the linkage programme was difficult to capture due to recall problem.
- If one selected the groups obtaining loan facility during 2002 and after, it was easier to meaningfully study the impact of interest on income and reinvestment.

The study, therefore, randomly selected 20 groups from among those who obtained loan facility from the banks during 2000 and 2001. These 20 groups were located in the same number of villages. Soon after reaching a village, a discussion with the available members of sample SHG was held. A list of members who had obtained NABARD loan was prepared to randomly select five members from among them. The information was collected from 100 members belonging to 20 groups and their representatives. The households were interviewed in their houses and in the local language by trained researchers. Interviews were also held with the managers of bank branches, which had provided credit facility to these SHGs. Bank officials were interviewed in the bank premises. The fieldwork was undertaken during the months of July and August 2003.

2

Micro-Finance Programme of Grama Vikas

The goal of Grama Vikas has been 'empowering marginalised rural women with special emphasis on children, natural resource management and networking with rural women's associations to accomplish sustainable development through food security'. Important activities initiated to achieve the objective of women development and empowerment are:

- savings and credit activities through the promotion of SHGs;
- income generation activities through community banking;
- linking SHGs with the banks to take up individual/community based activities, and influencing the policies of promotional agencies such as the National Bank for Agriculture and Rural Development (NABARD) in this regard;
- social action programmes;
- awareness and skill building programmes so as to strengthen their institutional capacity;
- dissemination of information of various government programmes;
- conducting training programmes and exposure visits;
- networking of women organisations at different levels; and
- discussing the issues related to women empowerment and development.

Grama Vikas covers 112 villages, of which 100 are in Mulbagal taluk, and the rest in Bangarpet taluk. These villages have been grouped into 15 clusters. The main project office is located in Honnesettihalli, which is 15 kms away from the taluk headquarters. The organisation had a total staff of 50 members in 2000. Only women had been recruited for all the programme activities. Among them, 15 were institutional development facilitators, 19 self-help facilitators, 11 administrators, 3 internal auditors and the rest were training and sector co-ordinators. Each cluster had one cluster organiser and one or two community organisers (depending on the size of the cluster) to carry out the various development activities.

Grama Vikas has been working with women, children and men from landless and marginal households belonging mainly to SC/ST categories. In 1998, the organisation had formed 172 SHGs for 3,790 women members (Table 1). Since the organisation worked with children and men belonging to the households of SHG members, the number of persons with whom the organisation worked was more than 3,790.

Table 1: Operational Details of Grama Vikas

Year	*No. of Villages Covered*	*No. of Clusters*	*No. of SHGs (Female Groups)*	*Target Group (Female)*
1996	104	15	114	3,488
1997	104	15	116	3,592
1998	112	15	172	3,790

Source: Data furnished by the Grama Vikas.

Women were organised into SHGs, each consisting of 11–18 members. They were formed for women mainly from landless and marginal farmer households belonging to SC, ST and backward castes. In each of the villages, there was at least one SHG and in some villages, there were 4–5 SHGs. The total number of SHGs in the project area of Grama Vikas increased from 114 in 1996 to 172 in 1998 (Table 1). By forming Parent's Federation, men were also encouraged to take up some community activities and play a supportive role to women SHG members. Men were also involved in development activities such as children's education and natural resource management activities (rehabilitation of tanks).

At the village level, Women's Samithis were formed in all the 104 villages. About 70 to 80 per cent of the target group women from the villages were members of the Women's Samithis. These members discussed various problems pertaining to themselves, some of which were girl children, environment, women's role in accomplishing food security and evolving appropriate means for their development.

Further, all the 104 women's Samithis together formed a people's organisation at the taluk level, called *Mahila Okkuta* (Women's Federation). This federation acts as an apex body to all the Women's Samithis in the project area. It also acts as a pressure group to mobilise and implement government programmes effectively through women's solidarity. Women's federation was delinked from the NGO, and was provided with its own staff, office and funds. This measure aimed at building long-term sustainability to the programme in the region.

Genesis of the Micro-Finance Programme

The organisation began with the feeding programme to rectify the nutritional imbalance among children and pregnant mothers with the help of donor funds. The sustainability of this programme was a great challenge to the organisation in the context of uncertain donor funding. Hence, introduction of small savings programme was considered as an essential component to sustain the feeding programme. Accordingly, poor women were encouraged to contribute small savings of Rs. 10 per month in the early 1990s. Simultaneously, the organisation initiated a credit programme under which loans from that of revolving credit fund set up through donor funds were advanced for agriculture and other income generation activities to enable the target group members to stabilise their income, and consume nutritious food on a sustainable basis.

Around this time, the representatives of the organisation participated in workshops on savings and credit organised by their principal donor agency of NOVIB. In these workshops, issues such as the need to revolve savings of the members as loans to enable them to develop social control mechanism were raised. Another issue that was raised was the strengthening of the capacity of the members in organising their own meetings, taking decisions on savings and credit activities and recovery of loans. In short, the need for building the capacity of the members in managing micro-finance programme was emphasised. It was also emphasised that there was a need to mobilise local resources (from government and banks) so that the target group members could obtain increased loan amounts on a regular basis. Influenced by the arguments in the workshop the organisation started savings and credit programmes from 1992 onwards. Preliminary efforts to form women's federation and entrusting it with some responsibilities in the management of savings and credit programme were started in 1994. Gradually, the capacity of the federation was enhanced to take on additional responsibilities.

The Grama Vikas facilitated the formation of mahila samithis (women organisations) in the initial years. These organisations were formed for the target group of poor women in the entire village. Typically, each mahila samithi consisted of 30 to 110 members. The average size was around 40. From mid-1990s, a decision was taken to divide larger samithis into smaller organisations and mould them as SHGs.

As far as the formation of new groups was concerned especially under the World Bank Programme of Swa-Shakthi, Grama Vikas was following a different methodology wherein participatory techniques were utilised and the target group members were involved in the formation. The *Mahila Okkuta* identified the village and requested the staff to conduct PRA exercises to identify the poor in a village or a locality. Subsequently, the members of *Mahila Okkuta* together with people took active part in deciding who among the poor in a village should be in the first SHG and who should be in the second SHG and so on.

Functioning of the Micro-Finance Programme

Each group in the project area had a President and Secretary, elected by the members. The members with greater awareness and mobility (i.e., the women who could spare time to travel to taluk headquarters and NGO project area) were elected as leaders in the first year. This practice was followed as a conscious strategy of stabilising the group in the first year. The mandatory rotation of leadership once a year was followed to enable all the members to get an opportunity to become group leaders. According to the organisation, rotation of leadership once a year was strictly followed in most of the groups. The functions of the leaders were as follows:

(a) conducting meetings;
(b) resolving conflicts among members;

(c) enabling the members to contribute savings and borrow from out of savings fund;
(d) depositing the savings in the bank and withdrawal when members needed loans from the savings fund;
(e) mobilising resources from the government and loans from the banks; and
(f) representing the group in the federation and acting as link between the group and *Mahila Okkuta*/NGO.

SHGs were expected to conduct two meetings in a month. However, the SHG members normally found it difficult to attend two meetings during the busy agricultural season. Hence, the groups decided that members could skip one of the meetings. But, organising at least one meeting in a month was essential. Whenever a new programme was to be planned and initiated, frequent interactions among members were needed and the groups met even four or more times in a month. The meetings were normally held at community centres, school buildings, and prayer centres. In the villages, where these facilities were not present, the members met in the houses of the group members.

In general, the staff from the NGO attended the meetings regularly if the group happened to be young. In the case of older groups, the staff attended only one of the meetings in a month. It may be noted here that Grama Vikas was following a withdrawal strategy wherein the role of the organisation gradually became facilitative, while that of SHGs and their federation was implementation. As a part of this strategy, the organisation constantly monitored the status of SHG. If the monitoring revealed that the group attained self-management capacity, the staff would not spend much time on basic aspects like facilitating the group meetings, etc. However, in those villages where there was a problem of finding a book-writer either from among members or from the village, the staff continued to play an active role in the preparation and maintenance of accounts and documents relating to the group.

Savings Programme

To begin with, each member was expected to contribute Rs. 10 per month. The amount of monthly savings was gradually raised to

Rs. 40 per month. The following institutional rules were formulated to ensure that savings amounts of individual members grew:

- Savings amount of an individual member was taken into consideration while disbursing a loan.
- The savings amount was not returned to a member so long as she was part of the SHG. Instead, a member could borrow from out of the savings fund for consumption and short-term production needs such as working capital for crop production, income generation activities, etc.
- The groups had to pay 10 per cent of interest on savings calculated once in six months. The accumulated interest amount was credited into the account of individual member whenever the group had funds.

The institutional rules seem to have had some impact on the accumulated amount of savings of all the members in the programme, which grew from Rs. 6,173 in 1990 to Rs.52.73 lakhs in 1999. The amount of savings per member was Rs.1,225 in 1999.

Lending Programme

A group member in the project area of Grama Vikas could take loans from: (i) savings fund, (ii) *Mahila Okkuta*, and (iii) banks through NABARD-SHG linkage programme. The strategy of making credit available from three sources for the members was based on the premise that credit needs of the poorer households differed. Poorer households required lumpy amounts for three types of needs: life-cycle (education, marriage, housing, etc.), emergencies (health, crop loss, droughts, accidents, etc.) and income generation. The strategy of Grama Vikas was to provide credit through savings fund for emergencies, education and, to some extent, working capital needs. Loans from *Mahila Okkuta* and banks were meant for income generation, and certain types of life-cycle needs such as housing and marriage.

The strategy of having three different sources of credit influenced the organisation to formulate institutional rules to curb the tendencies of free riding. The strategy of using credit as an instrument of poverty reduction and empowerment also necessitated the institutional rules. The organisation, therefore, formulated the following rules, and these rules were roughly the same across the three sources of credit.

- A person should have been a member in a group for a minimum period of six months before she could access credit from any of the sources. This rule would enable the group to obtain better information on a member before a loan was sanctioned. A member completing six months in a group could only take consumption loan from the groups' savings fund as the required savings amount might be too small to enable her to obtain a larger loan. Only when a member had savings in the range of Rs.1,000 to 3,000, could she obtain loan amount sufficient to undertake an income generation activity. Thus, in practice, the new members normally obtained loans from group funds and as the savings amount increased, they became gradually eligible to borrow from the federation or from a bank.
- The principle of savings linked to credit was followed. This meant that the savings amount of a member should be in a certain ratio of requested loan amount. The ratio varied from 1:2 in the case of consumption loans to 1:3 in the case of income generation loans. In the case of loans for house construction and purchase of land, the savings linked to credit was not strictly followed. The principle of savings linked to credit, in a way, conditioned the ability of the member to take loan from different sources. However, in exceptional and genuine cases, the savings linked to credit principle were relaxed so that they could obtain credit.
- Another condition was that a member borrowing from the federation should not have outstanding dues in the group or in a local bank.

The interest rate on all types of loans was 24 per cent per annum. It needs to be, however, noted that the interest rate on loans to SHGs under the bank-SHG linkage programme was 12.5 per cent. The groups, in any case, charged 24 per cent on the borrowing members and kept the difference in the interest amount for group related developmental activities. The same was the practice if the federation took a bulk loan from the banks for on-lending purposes. The interest amount earned by the groups was spent on development activities such as expenses incurred in connection with organising meetings, getting in touch with the officials to obtain resources for the groups, purchase of stationery, etc.

Description of Sample Villages

There is a considerable variation in the size of the village in terms of number of households and total population. The number of households in the villages varied from as low as 19 to as high as 815. Correspondingly, the total population also varied across the villages. The numerically dominant caste (accounting for over 50 per cent of the households in a village) was SC/ST community in eight villages, the forward castes (Vokkaliga and Reddy) in five villages and the backward castes (Kuruba, Golla and Agasa) in two villages. In five villages, the dominant caste group could not be ascertained as two or more caste groups were important.

In order to see the remoteness of sample villages, the distance between village and taluk headquarters was obtained. As Table 2 shows, only a few villages are located less than three kms away from the taluk headquarters. A majority of the villages are located at a distance of more than 10 kms away from the taluk headquarters.

The number of SHGs formed by the Grama Vikas and government varied from 1 to 4, and tended to be high in larger villages.

The primary school and mini water supply were the most commonly found government facilities in the villages. These were followed by milk co-operative society and community centre. The information, thus, shows that the villages had only basic minimum government facilities.

Due to uncertain rainfall in the taluk, a number of irrigation tanks had come into existence in the taluk to provide irrigation facility. Years of neglect and lack of state patronisation resulted in the ruin of these tanks, and emergence of well irrigation. The number of open and borewells rapidly increased in the last four decades. A rapid growth in the number of wells and lack of commensurate efforts in the rejuvenation of water harvesting structures resulted in the steady decline in the water table in the area, leading to well irrigation becoming gradually expensive and uncertain.

Table 2: Basic Characteristics of Sample Villages

Sl No	*Name of the Village*	*Households (%) Belonging to*				*Total Population of the Village*	*Distance (kms) to the Village from Taluk Headquarters*
		SC/ST	*Forward Caste*	*OBC*	*Total (in nos.)*		
1.	Batrahalli	41.7	40.3	18.1	72	538	8
2.	Beemanatha	43.8	10.9	45.3	64	357	18
3.	Bikkanahalli	33.3	29.6	37.0	135	380	17
4.	Chennapura	27.5	72.5	0.0	91	476	12
5.	D.Kurubarahalli	55.4	35.7	8.9	56	335	12
6.	Kadukachanahalli	25.4	44.8	29.9	67	431	9
7.	Kannatha	76.7	23.3	0.0	60	287	5
8.	Kappalamadagu	40.6	59.4	0.0	815	1,220	8
9.	Kodigenahalli	0.0	100.0	0.0	20	215	29
10.	Kumudenahalli	68.4	0.0	31.6	19	86	3
11.	Mallekuppa	59.8	29.9	10.3	117	612	17
12.	Moparahalli	74.2	25.8	0.0	132	688	18
13.	N.Kurubarahalli	31.3	14.1	54.7	64	348	15
14.	P.Gangapura	35.3	60.8	3.9	51	147	7
15.	Pitchguntlahalli	78.6	21.4	0.0	70	460	8
16.	Puliobareddihalli	70.4	22.5	7.0	71	457	11
17.	Pulipapenahalli	82.0	18.0	0.0	61	366	12
18.	Shettikal	28.1	45.8	26.1	153	792	15
19.	Vegamadagu	0.0	59.0	41.0	195	608	21
20.	Virupakshi	32.5	4.2	63.3	409	1,141	4

The important food crops cultivated in the area are ragi and paddy, while groundnut, vegetables, mulberry, mangoes and other horticultural crops are important commercial crops. Since the cultivation of commercial crops (except groundnut) is feasible and profitable on irrigated land, the cultivation of vegetables and mulberry has been undertaken by those farmers having access to irrigation. The groundnut crop is largely cultivated on rainfed lands, and hence, there is a considerable year-to-year variation in the productivity and income of the crop. Table 3 also shows that Ragi and Paddy are the crops grown in all the villages. Oil seeds and vegetables are other important cash crops. The cultivation of mulberry and sugarcane is also popular in a few villages.

Table 3: Number of SHGs, Facilities and Major Crops in the Sample Villages

Sl. No	*Name of the Village*	*No. of SHGs*	*Facilities in the Villages*	*Major Crops Grown*
1	Batrahalli	2	PS, MWS, MCS	Ragi, Paddy, Groundnut, Vegetables
2	Beemanatha	2	PS, MWS, MCS	Ragi, Paddy, Groundnut, Vegetables
3	Bikkanahalli	2	PS, MWS, MCS	Ragi, Paddy, Groundnut, Vegetables
4	Chennapura	4	PS, MWS, CC	Ragi, Paddy, Sugarcane, groundnut
5	D.Kurubarahalli	2	Anganawadi, PS, MWS, CC	Ragi, Paddy, Vegetables, Groundnut
6	Kadukachanahalli	2	PS, MWS, CC	Ragi, Paddy, Sugarcane, groundnut
7	Kannatha	1	PS, CC	Ragi, Paddy, Sericulture
8	Kappalamadagu	4	Anganawadi, PS, MS, GP, MWS, CC	Ragi, Paddy, Sericulture
9	Kodigenahalli	2	Anganawadi, PS, MS, MWS	Ragi, Groundnut, Paddy, Sericulture
10	Kumudenahalli	1	PS, MWS	Ragi, Paddy, Groundnut
11	Mallekuppa	4	PS, MWS, MCS	Ragi, Paddy, Groundnut, Vegetables
12	Moparahalli	3	PS, MWS, MCS	Ragi, Paddy, Groundnut, Vegetables
13	N.Kurubarahalli	1	PS, MWS, MCS	Ragi, Paddy, Groundnut, Vegetables
14	P.Gangapura	1	PS, MWS, MCS	Ragi, Paddy, Groundnut, Vegetables
15	Pitchguntlahalli	2	PS, MWS, MCS	Ragi, Paddy, Groundnut, Vegetables
16	Puliobareddihalli	3	Anganawadi, PS, MWS, CC, MCS	Ragi, Paddy, Sugarcane, Vegetables
17	Pulipapenahalli	2	PS, MCS, MWS, CC	Paddy, Sugarcane, groundnut, Ragi
18	Shettikal	2	Anganawadi, PS, MWS, CC	Ragi, Paddy, Groundnut
19	Vegamadagu	3	PS, MWS, MCS	Ragi, Paddy, Groundnut, Vegetables
20	Virupakshi	2	Anganawadi, PS, MS, MWS, MCS	Ragi, Paddy, Mulberry

Note: PS = Primary School, MS = Middle School, MWS = Mini Water Supply, CC = Community Centre, MCS = Milk Co-operative Society, GP = Grama Panchayat

Dairying is also an important activity in the area. With the establishment of Kolar Milk Federation, opening up of market routes and bank loans to rural households for undertaking the activity of rearing milch animals, dairying activity picked up very well in the area providing supplementary or substantial income to a significant proportion of the households in the taluk. In 12 out of 20 villages, the milk co-operative societies existed. This implies that marketing facilities were available to the households in a large number of villages.

The discussion on sample villages suggests the following. First, the sample SHGs were found in villages dominated by SC/ST and backward castes. This implies that the SHGs had been formed in poorer villages. Second, agriculture had depended on rainfall, and hence, crop production loans did not have favourable conditions. Yet, since the households did not have alternative credit sources, giving loans for crop production was justified. Third, marketing facilities for milk production made the loans for dairying viable.

Collaboration Between Grama Vikas and NABARD

Between 1994 and 2003, the organisation enabled its target group to obtain 2,736 loans from different banks, and a total loan amount of Rs.1.21 crores. Given that the total number of target group members were around 6,000, it could be suggested that nearly half of the target group households benefited from the banks (Tables 4 and 5) since the inception of the linkage programme.

The data on distribution of loans by the banks show interesting trends. In all, 15 branches of four different banks had provided assistance to SHGs formed by Grama Vikas. These were eight branches of Kolar Grameena Bank (KGB), three branches of Canara bank, three branches of State Bank of Mysore and one branch of Vijaya Bank. The KGB branches accounted for maximum proportion of loans and loan amount. The four KGB branches at M N Halli, Avani, Bhalla and Kashipura were important in extending finance to Grama Vikas groups, while the Mulbagal branch of the Canara bank and Nangli branch of the State Bank of Mysore were important among commercial banks.

The bank-SHG linkage programme can be seen in three phases:

initial phase (1994–95), middle phase (1996–2000) and latest phase (2001–03). A noteworthy feature about the relative importance of these bank branches is that a particular branch had played an important role in a particular phase. For instance, the branches of Avani, M N Halli and Bhalla were important RRBs during the middle phase. However, Kashipura and M N Halli were important during the latest phase, while the branches of Avani and Bhalla did not provide any assistance during the latest phase. In contrast, the Mulbagal branch of the Canara bank and the Nangali branch of the State Bank of Mysore remained important in all the three phases.

Table 4: Distribution (%) of Number of Loans by Different Banks

Name of the Bank	*Initial Phase (1994–95)*	*Middle Phase (1996–2000)*	*Latest Phase (2001–03)*	*Total (in Nos.)*
Regional Rural Banks				
Avani	23.2	76.8	0.0	327
Balla	18.8	81.3	0.0	176
MN Halli	8.2	36.5	55.3	790
Vadda Halli	0.0	13.6	86.4	88
Kashipura	0.0	0.0	100.0	184
Mulbagal	0.0	44.8	55.2	29
Sundara Palya	0.0	0.0	100.0	10
Bada Makana Halli	0.0	0.0	100.0	30
Canara Bank				
Mulbagal	13.0	53.5	33.5	523
Thayalur	20.7	79.3	0.0	29
Bethmangala	0.0	100.0	0.0	15
State Bank of Mysore				
Nangali	11.8	37.7	50.5	459
Kolar	0.0	0.0	100.0	38
Mulbagal	0.0	52.6	47.4	19
Vijaya Bank				
Devarayasamudra	100.0	0.0	0.0	19
Total	11.7	44.2	44.1	2,736

Table 5: Distribution (%) of Loan Amount by Different Banks

Name of the Bank	*Initial Phase (1994–95)*	*Middle Phase (1996–2000)*	*Latest Phase (2001–03)*	*Total (in Rs.)*
Regional Rural Banks				
Avani	9.0	91.0	0.0	1,365,000
Balla	8.5	91.5	0.0	971,700
MN Halli	6.1	53.0	40.9	3,907,700
Vadda Halli	0.0	9.4	90.6	287,000
Kashipura	0.0	0.0	100.0	966,000
Mulbagal	0.0	60.3	39.7	235,600
Sundara Palya	0.0	0.0	100.0	43,800
Bada Makana Halli	0.0	0.0	100.0	125,000
Canara Bank				
Mulbagal	7.2	70.7	22.1	2,276,400
Thayalur	12.2	87.8	0.0	180,000
Bethmangala	0.0	100.0	0.0	14,500
State Bank of Mysore				
Nangali	12.0	50.9	37.1	1,550,000
Kolar	0.0	0.0	100.0	60,000
Mulbagal	0.0	20.4	79.6	113,000
Vijaya Bank				
Devarayasamudra	100.0	0.0	0.0	25,000
Total	6.9	57.5	35.6	12,120,700

The loan amount provided to a member in a group also varied across the three phases (Table 6). Between 1994 and 2003, 246 groups in the project area of Grama Vikas benefited from NABARD bank linkage programme. In the initial phase, the amount of bank loan for each member ranged between Rs.5,000 and 6,000 in the case of nearly 38 per cent of the groups. In the middle phase also, the loan amount for each member varied between Rs.5,000 and 10,000 in about 50 per cent of the groups. However, in the latest phase, the proportion of groups obtaining higher average amounts declined to 24 per cent. In the case of 45 per cent of the groups, the average amount of loan for each member was less than Rs.3,000. This implies that either the amount disbursed by the banks to each group had declined or the number of members in a group had gone up. An examination of the data shows that the amount of loan provided by the banks to groups declined in recent years.

Table 6: Distribution of SHGs (%) by Per Member Loan Amount

Per Member Loan Amount (in Rs.)	*Initial Phase (1994–95)*	*Middle Phase (1996–2000)*	*Latest Phase (2001–03)*	*Total*
<2,000	34.3	4.4	45.1	25.3
2,000 – 5,000	27.5	48.7	30.7	38.6
5,000 – 10,000	34.4	37.7	22.1	30.5
Above 10,000	3.4	9.7	1.9	5.7
Total	100.0 (29)	100.0 (113)	100.0 (104)	100.0 (246)

Note: Figures in parentheses are actual number of groups obtaining loans in each phase.

There were also variations across phases in so far as the purpose for which NABARD loans were provided (Table 7). Of the 321 loans disbursed in the initial phase, nearly 90 per cent was given for undertaking income generating activities relating to dairying and livestock rearing. Of the 1,208 loans disbursed in the middle phase, dairying and livestock accounted for about 61 per cent. The proportion of loans given for irrigation development, agriculture (crop production, etc) and housing registered a significant increase.

Table 7: Distribution of NABARD Loans (%) for Different Purposes During the Phases

Name of the Activity	*Initial Phase (1994–95)*	*Middle Phase (1996–2000)*	*Latest Phase (2001–03)*	*Total*
Agriculture	4.4	12.7	22.5	15.2
Dairying	38.9	38.4	21.4	32.2
Livestock	51.4	23.0	39.1	32.7
Irrigation	1.6	17.6	0.2	9.1
Land purchase	0.9	1.7	0.6	1.2
Non-Agricultural activities	0.6	1.7	5.8	3.1
Marriages, consumption and health	0.3	0.2	1.3	0.6
Housing	1.6	4.7	3.8	4.0
Loan recovery	0.0	0.0	5.0	1.9
Others	0.3	0.0	0.2	0.1
Total	100.0 (321)	100.0 (1,208)	100.0 (896)	100.0 (2,425)

Note: Figures in parentheses are actual number of groups obtaining loans in each phase.

In the third phase, the proportion of loans disbursed to undertake (both construction and repair) dairying and livestock declined marginally. Those given for agriculture and non-agricultural activities registered a significant increase. Interestingly, the proportion of loans given to recover the old loans under the bank-SHG programme was five per cent in the latest phase (2001–03). The data, thus, show that the portfolio of loans under NABARD bank-SHG linkage witnessed significant changes in the last one decade. The importance of dairying and livestock declined, while that of agriculture, irrigation development and non-agriculture activity increased.

Five per cent of the loans given for the purpose of repayment of previous loan in the latest phase implies that SHGs, NGO and banks could not recover a sizeable proportion of loans, and hence, had to be rescheduled. This also implies that the members were finding it difficult to repay the loans on account of a number of factors. Is interest rate on NABARD loans one of the factors? If yes, how significant is this? We take up these questions for discussion later.

3

Transaction Costs to Bank Branches

Of the fifteen bank branches which had provided financial assistance to SHGs in the project area of Grama Vikas, eight had provided loans to the sample SHGs. The study team interviewed all the managers of the banks except the KGB, Kumudenahalli. The following discussion is, therefore, confined to seven bank branches.

Of the seven bank branches, three belonged to commercial banks and four to RRBs. The number of villages in the service area ranged from as low as 24 in the case of Canara Bank, Mulbagal, to as high as 62 in the case of State Bank of Mysore, Nangli (Table 8). The lower number of villages in the case of the former is probably due to the fact that this bank branch is located in Mulbagal town. The number of SHGs supported by the bank ranged from a low of 3 in KGB, Avani, to a high of 92 in the case of SBM, Nangli. Consequently, the ratio of SHGs to villages covered by the sample bank branches also varied across the villages. Thus, it was not that all the banks were actively participating in the linkage programme.

The total amount of deposits and outstanding loan amount by the sample banks also differed. The Canara Bank, Mulbagal, being a semi-urban bank, had high level of deposits and outstanding loan amount. On the other hand, the KGB, Kashipura, had the lowest level of deposits and outstanding loan amount among the sample bank branches. The credit-deposit ratio was the highest in the case of KGB, Vaddahalli, followed by SBM, Nangli, and KGB, Kashipura. Although data were not available for all the bank branches, it can be concluded that the credit-deposit ratio was higher in the case of RRBs. The total amount of outstanding loan to SHGs as a proportion of the total outstanding loan in the bank branch was negligible in the case of all the sample bank branches. This indicates that there was some scope to increase the bank-linkage programme in the area covered by sample bank branches.

Table 8: Basic Details of Sample Banks

Name of the Bank	*Number of Villages in the Service Area*	*Total Amount of Deposits (in Rs. Crores)*	*Outstanding Loan Amount (in Rs. Crores)*	*Credit Deposit Ratio*	*Number of SHGs Assisted by the Bank*	*Total Amount (Rs.) of Assistance Provided to SHGs*
Canara Bank, Mulbagal	24	6.73	4.03	0.60	37	1,822,000
KGB, Avani	39	2.11	1.52	0.72	3	575,000
Canara Bank, Tayaloor	30	NA	NA	NA	10	1,400,000
KGB, Vaddahalli	24	2.22	2.32	1.05	29	820,600
SBM, Nangli	62	3.90	4.05	1.04	92	823,000
KGB, Kashipura	26	1.04	1.04	1.00	16	900,000
KGB, Mallanayakanahalli	38	2.63	NA	NA	38	1,846,000

Note: NA—Not available

The total amount of loan provided to each SHG was substantial in the case of a large proportion of the sample SHGs. Only one SHG was given less than Rs. 10,000. While five SHGs were given loans in the range of Rs. 10,000 to 25,000, seven were given loans in the range of Rs. 25,000 to 50,000. Five SHGs were given loans in the range of Rs. 50,000 to 100,000. The number of SHGs obtaining more than Rs. 100,000 was two.

What is the transaction cost to the bank branches? This question is difficult to answer with the supportive quantitative data as the information was not separately maintained for the linkage programme. Hence, qualitative data have been analysed below to obtain a general picture on transaction costs and how they compared with other types of loans. Since the number of visits to the SHGs, training, paper work and supervision influenced the transaction costs, these have been examined below.

Number of Visits

Given that the amounts lent by the banks to each SHG were substantial, the discussion on the type of screening process adopted by the bank branches and the number of visits undertaken by the staff becomes important. The bank managers stated that in the case of 16 out of 20 sample SHGs, the number of visits made was between two and three (Table 9). It was stated that one visit was made before sanctioning the loan, one visit after the sanction and one visit if there was any problem with regard to repayment. The bank managers stated that visits to two SHGs were not undertaken at all.

Table 9: Distribution of Groups by Number of Visits by Bank Officials

No. of Visits According to the SHGs	*No. of Visits According to the Bankers*					*Total*
	None	*Once*	*Twice*	*Thrice*	*NA*	
None	1	0	3	2	2	8
Once	1	0	3	0	0	4
Twice	0	0	3	4	0	7
Thrice	0	0	0	1	0	1
Total	2	0	9	7	2	20

Note: NA—Not available

The SHG representatives contradicted the statements of bank managers on the number of visits. The representatives of as many as eight SHGs stated that the bank staff never visited their groups. Four of them stated that the bank staff visited their groups once, while seven of them stated that the staff visited their groups twice. The number of SHGs stating that the bankers visited their groups three times was only one.

Whose version on the number of visits by the bank staff to SHGs is correct? Answer to this question is to be found in the qualitative information provided by the bankers, SHG representatives and the criteria followed in the selection of SHGs for assistance.

- The responses of the bank staff on the number of visits indicated that the information was incorrect. The opening sentence in most of the cases was that the visits were not needed; and, afterthought, they came up with some figure. In some cases, the manager had been recently posted and hence, did not know the number of visits. In such cases, the manager provided the figure on the basis of general pattern; in other words, he stated that, in general, one visit each would be undertaken before, after and during the repayment.

- The representatives of eight SHGs were very certain that the bank staff did not visit them at all. They noted that despite their repeated requests to visit the group, the bank staff did not visit the group. The responses were 'there is no need', 'you bring all the documents here for an examination' and 'it is alright if your NGO guarantees the loan'. The representatives also stated that the visits were made only in those cases where the bank did not have previous experience of lending to the groups, or the new manager did not have previous experience. According to a few articulate representatives, there was no compelling reason for the bankers to visit the group since they, in any case, obtained good information from the periodicity and amount of savings deposited in the bank, and regular visits to the bank by SHG representatives to deposit the savings.
- The basis on which the sample banks disbursed loans to SHGs also provided some clues on the number of visits. It needs to be noted that the NABARD has developed a format to assess the status of SHG before the loan is sanctioned. The criteria used to assess SHG include the performance of the group in meetings, savings, maintenance of accounts, internal circulation of money, repayment of loans, etc. Even then, most of the bank managers noted that the savings amount together with guarantees by the NGO and internal circulation of savings determined the decision to lend to a group. This suggests that the decision-making behaviour of the branch managers in the case of SHG loans was similar to that of the other loans. In other words, the collateral security was the main yardstick used by the branch managers, and savings and guarantees of NGOs had served the purpose of collateral security. Since the savings amount was kept in the bank, there was no need for the bankers to visit the group.

Since the number of visits was nil or one to two in most of the cases, the transaction costs on account of number of visits were not substantial to the bank branches.

Training to SHG Members

Did the bank staff provide training to SHG members? The responses from the bank managers show that none of them provided any training to SHG members as it was generally perceived that the responsibility of providing training was vested with the NGO. This was further corroborated by the responses of SHG representatives. The representatives of nine out of 12 SHGs that were visited by the bank managers stated that the purpose of the visit was to inspect the SHG by verifying the records. Only one of the SHGs noted that the bank staff provided them awareness on bank loans and the need to repay the loan amount promptly. Thus, the banks did not spend any money on training the SHG members.

Paper Work

All the bank managers noted that the bank-SHG linkage programme had, to a large extent, contributed to reduced paper work (Table 10). An overwhelming response was that a single document was sufficient for about 20 members in a group. Further, the NGO staff attended to all the documentation work, and hence, the banks did not spend any time on preparing the documents also. Thus, the transaction costs in the case of bank-SHG linkage programme were minimal, and considerably lower as compared to other bank lending programmes such as crop loans, agricultural gold loans and term loans.

Supervision Costs

Four bank managers stated that there was a significant reduction in the supervision costs under the bank-SHG linkage programme, while two of them perceived that there was only partial reduction. One of them did not provide any response. The reasons attributed for the decline in supervision costs have been provided below:

- There was no need to contact all the members individually as the representatives frequently came to the bank to deposit the savings.
- The NGO staff supervised, and hence, there was no need to undertake supervision visits.
- The above imply that there was less number of visits and follow up leading to saving of time and manpower.

- Some bankers stated that there was minimal or no supervision at all.
- Even if one were to undertake supervision visits, the SHG provided an opportunity to the bank to have all the members assembled at one place, and to have an interaction with them.

All these factors imply that the costs incurred towards supervision were minimal or non-existent.

Table 10: Responses of Bankers on Costs Incurred in the Bank-SHG Llinkage Programme

Attributes	*To a Large Extent*	*Par-tially*	*No Res-ponse*	*Explanation for the Responses*
Reduced paper work	7	0	0	• One document for nearly 20 members. • NGO did the documentation. For other loans, the bank had to collect data.
Reduced super-vision cost	4	2	1	• Reduced supervision since NGO took care of the activities. • Less follow up and manpower saving. • Less visits, reduced cost of recovery and time saving. • No need to contact all the members. • Minimum supervision – no supervision at all. • NGOs supervised. • Since NGOs formed SHGs, they saw to it that loan was used for the purpose for which it was taken. • All were available at one place.
Improved recovery of loans given to poorer sections	5	1	1	• The rate of recovery in the SHG programme was 50 per cent, while it was only 20 per cent in the other programmes. • Recovery in the private loans was 65 per cent and in SHGs it was 98 per cent. • Less effort in the recovery. • NGOs took the responsibility.

Loan Recovery

According to five bank managers, the loan recovery had improved, to a large extent, under the bank-SHG linkage programme, while one bank manager stated that the loan recovery was partially better under the programme. Some of the bank managers provided figures showing that there was substantial difference between the bank-SHG linkage programme and other programmes in so far as the recovery was concerned. They attributed the difference to the responsibility undertaken by the NGO. Thus, although the bankers did not incur any significant costs towards training, selection and monitoring of the borrowers, the recovery rates were significantly higher under the programme.

In conclusion, it can be stated that the sample banks were faced with win-win situation in so far as the linkage programme was concerned. They provided loans to a large number of poor in the service area with minimum costs towards selection and supervision. In the process, they were able to save time and human resources, on the one hand, and to obtain good recovery rates and profitability in the whole operation, on the other.

Is the rate of interest charged by the banks sufficient to cover the cost of lending or more than the cost of lending? The responses to this question were non-committal from most of the bank managers. A couple of them noted that they did not have any response, while two of them stated that the rates were fixed by the Reserve Bank of India. One of them tried to convince us that the cost of raising funds was quite high. When it was stated that lending under bank-SHG programme was refinanced by NABARD and interest rates had been slashed down to about 5 per cent, he looked very uncomfortable. Three bank managers, however, noted that the rate of interest was more than the cost of lending, and the apex bank could reduce the interest rate by 1–3 per cent. One of these managers, however, stated that there was a case for only one per cent reduction as the lending was indirect, and there was no direct collateral in the programme.

4

Transaction Costs to SHGs

As in the case of the banks, SHGs also incur costs before, during and after obtaining the loans. In general, SHGs incur costs on the following:

- Travel and boarding costs in connection with visits to the banks for finding out whether they can avail the loan facility, submission of application form, follow-up, receiving the loan amount and for repayment.
- The costs on account of wage income foregone in connection with the visits.
- Hospitality costs in connection with the visits by bank officials.
- Purchase of stamp paper and other documentation.
- Time spent by members of SHGs in connection with selection, monitoring and repayment of loans.
- Default costs.

In order to cover these costs, the SHGs lend amounts obtained from the banks at 24 per cent, although they receive the loan from the banks at 12.5 per cent. Thus, the SHGs are expected to cover their costs with the interest amount of 11.5 per cent. It needs to be examined whether the SHGs have been successful in meeting the costs.

For working out the transaction costs incurred by the SHGs, data were collected from 20 SHGs located in different villages. Nearly half of the groups had been formed during 1992 to 1994, while eight of them had been formed in 2000. By July 2003, 12 groups had obtained loans from the banks once, seven groups twice and one of them as many as four times. The study, however, considered only those loans which were obtained during 2000 and 2001. As can be expected, most of the groups obtained the last loan from the banks in 2000 and 2001, while six of them obtained in 2002 and 2003.

Who provided information to SHGs in so far as linkage-banking was concerned? This question becomes important because linkage-banking programme aims to alleviate poverty. If that is the case, it can be expected that banks are required to provide information on linkage-banking to SHGs formed in the area as they are potential clients. Did banks spend resources (human and financial) in propagating the programme? When the question of who provided the information on SHG-Bank linkage programme was posed to the sample SHGs, almost all of them stated that they came to know about the programme through the NGO staff. This again shows that banks did not spend any resource and incur costs in propagating the programme, and were faced with win-win situation in this regard.

The total amount obtained by each SHG from the bank has varied. A few of the SHGs obtained more than Rs.1 lakh, while others obtained less than Rs.20,000. The rate of interest charged by the banks was 12.5 per cent. NABARD and the banks were of the opinion that the linkage-banking programme was advantageous to SHG members as the interest rate was low. The important questions in this regard are: Are SHGs able to obtain loans with only interest as cost? What are the other costs that they have incurred? How prominent are these costs?

The costs of getting loan from the banks under NABARD's bank-SHG linkage programme were not just confined to interest rates. The SHGs incurred expenses on travel, paper work and also on visiting bank officials in a few cases. We have also included the wage income foregone on account of visits to the bank branches. These aspects have been further discussed below.

Getting in Touch with the Bank

Data were collected from the Presidents/Vice Presidents of 20 groups in the sample villages. More than 50 per cent of the groups had visited the banks four or more times to receive the loans (Table 11). Twenty-five per cent of the groups said that they kept visiting the bank for over a month to get the loan sanctioned. Only 5 per cent of the groups said that they had visited the bank twice to avail the loan.

The duration between application and sanction of the loan varied from one month to four months. The delay in sanctioning the loans was due to the bank procedures to be followed before sanctioning the loans to SHG. After receiving the application from the SHG, the bank undertook SHG visit to know about its working condition. Once the bank was convinced, then the paper work like readying bond paper, obtaining signatures from the members, etc., began. The proportion of loan amount depended on the amount of group savings. If the group maintained good rapport with the bank, then the loan was sanctioned without delay. Another reason for the delay could be non-cooperation by the branch bank managers, who did not encourage the SHG members approaching them frequently and bringing unnecessary pressure for sanctioning the loans. This was because of the lack of awareness about the importance of SHGs in credit and savings activities.

The purpose of the first visit in the case of 30 per cent of the groups was to find out whether they were eligible to obtain loan from the bank. This shows that although the SHGs came to know about the linkage programme, they were still not certain of getting the loan. This resulted in a visit, and in the process, expenditure of money and wastage of time.

Around 40 per cent of the groups visited more than twice to follow up their applications. Lack of awareness on various steps involved in the SHG-Bank linkage programme resulted in the frequent follow-up. Further, the attitude of the banks also resulted in larger number of visits. The bank officials had often asked the group members to come again as they were either not ready to discuss about the application and/ or were not free to spend any time with the groups.

The banks would not give loans without the signature of ***Okkuta*** President. The Group members were sent back to get the signature of the *Okkuta* President. In some cases, the bank people asked the groups to get the clearance or sponsorship letter from Grama Vikas.

Sometimes, the bank officials asked the group members to bring all the records to the bank instead of the bank officials themselves visiting the groups.

In addition to this, the banks would not provide loans to the group, if any person from the household of the group member happened to be a defaulter during the IRDP programme period. Until the repayment of such personal loans, the group members had to visit the banks frequently. The groups, in such cases, had to choose between making such households repay the overdue loan or foregoing the loans under the Bank-SHG linkage programme. The sample SHGs chose to convince the members to repay the overdue amounts. This was often difficult for SHG leaders and women members. The latter had to talk to their spouses, who were not convinced as they were of the opinion that the loans were waived by the Union government in 1990. This again resulted in more number of visits to the banks.

Table 11: Purpose of Visiting the Bank

	First visit	*Second Visit*	*Third Visit*	*Fourth Visit*
To find out whether loan can be given	6	0	0	0
To give application	10	7	2	0
To bring application	1	0	0	0
Follow up	0	7	8	2*
To give linkage format	0	1	0	0
Taking records to the bank for verification	0	1	0	0
To receive the loan	0	1	5	9
For signing	0	0	1	0
Gave application and obtained loan	3	0	0	0
Obtained loans	0	3	4	9
Total	20	20	20	20

* Obtained loans in the fifth and sixth visit, respectively.

Costs in Establishing the Linkage

Since the banks were not located in the sample villages, the SHG members had to travel to other villages where the banks were located. In the case of about 50 per cent of the sample villages, the distance to banks was more than 5 kms. In the case of some of the villages, SHG members had to travel for 20 kms as there was no direct bus service. Since there was no proper communication between the banks and SHGs, the members were asked to visit the banks frequently and as a consequence the cost of establishing the linkage had gone up. In general, the members walked to the bank branches if the latter were located at a distance of less than 2 kms. If the bank branch was located at a distance of more than 2 kms, the members had to take the local transportation such as bus, auto, etc. The number of visits was invariably more than two in most of the cases due to the following reasons:

- The members had to enquire whether the loan provision existed in the concerned bank branch.
- To bring the application.
- To submit the application after it was duly filled.
- An additional visit became necessary if the concerned bank officer was not present when the members visited the bank.
- Despite that the NGO made all efforts to build the capacity of the members, widespread illiteracy and anxiety on the part of the SHG members resulted in additional visits.
- The bank officials frequently asked the members to come again.
- The bank officials, in some cases, asked for a kind of recommendation letter from Grama Vikas, which was used as collateral security.
- Some bank officials asked the SHG members to bring all the records to the bank instead of they themselves visiting the group as per the norms.
- Some bank managers compelled all the members to be present at the bank while the loan was sanctioned to the group. This resulted in considerable expenditure on travel.

The travel costs in the case of Bheemanatha SHG were higher at Rs. 1,600, and nil in N. Kurubarahalli. The travel costs in the case of the former were high on account of both distance and larger number of visits by larger number of members. The lower costs in the case of villages such as N. Kurubarahalli were on account of location of the bank branch close to the village. Thus, both distance, number of visits and number of members visiting the bank influenced the total transportation costs.

Further, the cost on paper work was also more. For submitting the application the members had to incur expenses. The banks would not provide loans without bond papers as the members had to submit bonds with the signatures of all the members. The information obtained from the audited accounts of SHGs show that the cost of bond paper ranged from Rs.80 to 200 depending on the amount of loan that the members obtained from the bank.

Another important component in the total costs incurred by SHGs was the wage income foregone. The discussions with SHG members revealed that they could not attend to their work if they had to visit the bank located far from the village. The travel by bus took time, and they had to be present in the bank during the transaction hours. Further, the bank officials made them wait for about 30 minutes to two hours. All this meant that they had lost nearly one day. If the bank branch was located close to the village, the members spent only half-a-day.

Based on the above, the wage income foregone was estimated. In the case of the villages distantly located from the bank branch, one full-day was taken into account, and if the bank branch was located close to the village half-a-day was taken. Since the average wage was Rs.30 (Rs.35 during the peak season and Rs.25 during the off-season), the study worked out the wage income foregone by taking Rs.30 as the wage per day.

Table 12 shows that the total wage income foregone was Rs.1,080 in Bheemanatha and Rs.60 in Kodigenahalli. The variations in the total wage income foregone were on account of distance to the bank and total number of visits to the bank by all the members.

In addition to this, sometimes the members had to meet the expenditure on refreshments when the bank officials visited the village for studying and verification of records. In the case of 12 groups, Bank officials visited the groups at least once and in the case of 7 groups they visited more than once. The Bank officials visited groups in two periods, i.e., pre-sanction period and post-sanction period. At the time of visits, the officials conducted a sort of interview with the groups, and asked questions such as whether the members knew the purpose of savings. They also enquired whether the members had any clear-cut views on the purpose for which loan was going to be utilised. The banks agreed to provide the loan if the level of savings was high, and repayment of loans from savings fund was prompt.

Table 12: Distance and Cost in Establishing the Linkage

Sl No.	*Village*	*Name and Place of the Bank Linked*	*Distance to the Bank*	*Total No. of Members Visited*	*Total Paper Work*	*Total Transport Cost (Rs.)*	*Total Amount of Wages Foregone (Rs.)*
1	Pulipapenahalli	KGB, MN Halli	2	24	135	210	360
2	D.Kurubarahalli	KGB, MN Halli	2	22	155	55	330
3	Moparahalli	KGB, MN Halli	3	12	135	140	180
4	Beemanatha	KGB, MN Halli	3	72	200	1,600	1,080
5	Kadukatchanahalli	Canara bank, Mulbagal	10	68	200	272	660
6	Bikkanahalli	KGB, MN Halli	4	24	150	96	330
7	Vegamadagu	KGB, MN Halli	7	7	150	500	120
8	P. Gangapura	Canara bank, Mulbagal	6	17	150	68	510
9	N.Kurubarahalli	SBM, Nangali	1	26	150	0	360
10	Virupakshi	KGB, Avani	6	11	130	110	240
11	Batrahalli	KGB, Vaddahalli	5	6	154	240	120
12	Kumudenahalli	KGB, Mulbagal	25	23	130	138	570
13	Chennapura	KGB, Kashipura	4	10	100	100	240
14	Kannetha	KGB, Avani	8	8	150	200	180
15	Kappalamodagu	KGB, Vaddahalli	6	8	160	28	180
16	Pitchguntlahalli	Canara bank, Mulbagal	10	19	178	72	480
17	Kodigenahalli	Canara Bank, Tayaloor	10	30	150	360	60
18	Shettikal	SBM, Nangali	20	5	130	200	150
19	Puliobareddihalli	KGB, MN Halli	8	8	180	50	120
20	Mallekoppa	SBM, Nangali	2	25	200	40	420

The data show that in 66.7 per cent of the groups, the bank officials had not visited after the sanction of the loan. Even if the officials had visited during the post-sanction period, it was mainly for asking repayment in case there was no good repayment from the groups. Only in one village the bank officials verified whether the assets were purchased or not. If the group was not able to clear the loan, the bank officials visited the group for the purpose of renewal of the loan. This shows that involvement of the bank officials was low in the disbursement of loans and recovery of loans from the SHGs. Since the number of visits was small, the expenses incurred were either low or non-existent in most of the cases (Table 13).

Total Transaction Cost

The cost to SHGs in obtaining loan from the bank should be in the range of 11 per cent because this is the interest charged by the banks. Thus, if one includes only interest as cost to the SHGs, the total transaction cost as a proportion of total amount borrowed should not be more than 11 per cent. There is, however, a problem relating to the repayment status. The costs incurred are final only in the case of those loans which have been fully repaid. On the other hand, the costs in the case of those loans which are being repaid are not final and may change when a loan is completely repaid. In our sample, there were six SHGs which had completely repaid the loan to the banks, while two of them had repaid most of the amount. As many as 12 SHGs had only partially repaid the loan amount to the banks (Table 13). We, therefore, analysed the transaction costs separately for each of these categories.

As could be expected, the transaction costs were high for the SHGs which had fully repaid the loan. The proportion of transaction costs to total amount borrowed ranged from as low as 13.62 per cent in Pitchguntlahalli to as high as 43.69 per cent in Bikkanahalli in the case of those groups which had completely repaid the loan. This meant that the SHG members in Bikkanahalli spent as much as Rs.44 for every Rs.100 that they borrowed from the bank. Of the six groups which had repaid their loans two incurred more than Rs.20 for every Rs.100 borrowed from the bank.

When it came to the groups, which had repaid almost the whole amount, the proportion ranged from 12.54 per cent to 14.18 per cent. In the case of 12 groups, which had partially repaid their loan amount, the proportion of transaction costs to total amount borrowed ranged from as low as 11 per cent to as high as 26.67 per cent. The transaction cost in the case of groups which were yet to repay their loan amount might go up when they completely repay their loan amount.

It should also be noted that the cost to the SHG would be even high, if one included the default amount. In the case of a few groups, although the loan amount to the bank was completely repaid, a few members were still defaulters at the time of the survey. These members might repay in future. If they did not repay, the SHG would have to bear this loss. If we include the currently defaulted amount, the costs to each of the SHG would be higher than what is shown in Table 13. However, this information could not be systematically collected from all the groups.

Table 13: Total Transaction Costs to SHGs

Village	*Total Amount Borrowed (Rs.)*	*Expenses on Paper Work (Rs.)*	*Expenses on Transport (Rs.)*	*Total Wage Income Foregone (Rs.)*	*Expenses in Connection with Visits of Bankers (Rs.)*	*Interest Paid to the Bank (Rs.)*	*Total Cost Including Interest (Rs.)*	*Costs (%) to Total Loan Amount*	*Total Expenses (Rs.) (3+4+5+6)*	*Col. 10 as Percentage to Total Loan Amount Borrowed*
1	2	3	4	5	6	7	8	9	10	11
				Fully Repaid						
Kadukatchanahalli	15,000	200	272	660	20	1,473	2,625	17.50	1152	7.68
Bikkanahalli	44,000	150	96	330	0	18,646	19,222	43.69	576	1.31
Vegamadagu	23,500	150	500	120	0	2,831	3,601	15.32	770	3.28
Kannetha	64,000	150	200	180	0	17,493	18,023	28.16	530	0.83
Pitchguntlahalli	21,000	178	72	480	0	2,130	2,860	13.62	730	3.48
Mallekoppa	36,000	200	40	420	0	5,357	6,017	16.71	660	1.83
				Repaid Most of the Amount						
N.Kurubarahalli	36,000	150	0	360	0	4,005	4,515	12.54	510	1.42
Kodigenahalli	33,100	150	360	60	40	4,082	4,692	14.18	610	1.84
				Partially Repaid						
Pulipapenahalli	69,500	135	210	360	20	8,400	9,125	12.09	725	1.04
D.Kurubarahalli	132,000	155	55	330	0	14,472	15,012	11.37	540	0.41
Moparahalli	24,000	135	140	180	0	3,372	3,827	15.95	455	1.90
Beemanatha	126,000	200	1600	1080	0	17,520	20,400	16.19	2880	2.29
P. Gangapura	18,000	150	68	510	0	2,324	3,052	16.96	728	4.04
Virupakshi	49,500	130	110	240	0	6,766	7,246	14.64	480	0.97
Batrahalli	36,000	154	240	120	300	7,862	8,676	24.10	814	2.26
Kumudenahalli	90,000	130	138	570	0	10,115	10,953	12.17	838	0.93
Chennapura	25,800	100	100	240	0	2,683	3,123	12.10	440	1.71
Kappalamodagu	33,000	160	28	180	20	8,412	8,800	26.67	388	1.18
Shettikal	77,300	130	200	150	0	9,010	9,490	12.28	480	0.62
Puliobareddihalli	64,000	180	50	120	0	10,380	10,730	16.77	350	0.55

Selection, Monitoring and Enforcing Repayment

The process of selecting the beneficiaries for the Bank-SHG linkage programme was done in SHG meetings. Selection of the beneficiaries was largely done by the group (90 per cent) and partially by the *Mahila Okkuta* (10 per cent). The selection of the beneficiary depended upon the amount of savings, regular attendance and the immediate requirement of the loan. The proportion of the loan amount depended on the amount of savings in the ratio of 1:3. In some cases, the loan amount was equally distributed among the beneficiaries. The group also assessed the capability of the beneficiaries to repay the loan before the disbursal. Once the loan was disbursed among the members, necessary steps were undertaken to ensure that the credit was utilised for undertaking the activities. The staff made frequent visits to the beneficiary's house for inspection and also enquired with other people in the village. It was also mentioned that whenever the group came across mis-utilisation of the loan amount, it asked the beneficiaries to return the loan amount immediately. But, in practice, this did not happen. For instance, in one of the villages, the respondent obtained loan for the purchase of a gas stove whereas the record showed crossbred calf. This showed lack of monitoring. In order to make the members successful in undertaking the economic activity, the staff held frequent discussions, provided guidance, awareness about the insurance, solutions for the problems, etc. (Table 14). Sometimes, this was not possible for the group, as some of the beneficiaries would have experienced loss of economic activity like the death of livestock animals, crops drying up due to no rainfall, etc.

Table 14: Methods by Which Repayment Was Ensured by Sample SHGs

Methods	*Percentage of SHGs Following Different Ways (N=20)*
Insurance was made mandatory	10.0
Problems faced by the members were discussed and solutions were offered	20.0
The activities having success potential were selected	20.0
Group didn't follow any method	50.0
Total	100.0

In some of the villages, one could notice the regular repayment of loans. This was possible mainly due to the pressure from the bank officials on the staff, who, in turn, pressurised the members and also the members had the desire to avail the loan for the second time as there was a rule 'no second loan will be disbursed until the previous loan is repaid'. Some of the reasons for irregular repayment were unfavourable village conditions, low household income and loss in the economic activity. This increased the total interest amount paid to the bank, and hence, the total costs of the SHG in the linkage banking. If one were to include the costs on time spent by group members in the selection, monitoring and repayment, the costs would go up further.

Lack of data on default costs and time spent by SHG members in the selection, monitoring and repayment makes the analysis on the total costs of SHG incomplete. But, the indications are that the SHGs incurred more costs than what interest spread of 11.5 per cent would allow for. This is one of the reasons why most of the members felt that the SHG spent more than what was obtained from the members in the form of interest income.

5

Impact of Interest Rate on Income and Reinvestment

As noted in chapter 1, 5 households from each sample SHG were randomly selected in the presence of SHG members for canvassing the household questionnaire. The total number of sample households was 100. The proportion of households belonging to SC and ST communities was 53 per cent while those belonging to backward castes was 35 per cent. The rest belonged to forward castes such as Vokkaliga and Reddy.

Most of the sample households were landless, marginal and small farmers. The proportion of marginal farmers (less than 1 acre of land) was 34 per cent while the proportion of small farmers (between 1 to 2.5 acres of land) was 24 per cent. About 27 per cent of the households were medium farmers owning 3 to 5 acres of land.

Most of the households lived in *pucca* and semi-*pucca* houses. While households living in pucca houses mostly came from backward castes, those living in *kutcha* houses belonged to SC and ST communities.

The sample households obtained membership in the SHGs formed by Grama Vikas during the period 1990–2000. Over half of them joined their SHGs between 1990 and 1999, while 47 per cent of them joined in 2000 (Table 15). The reason why most of the

Table 15: Distribution (%) of Households by Year of Joining the Group

Year of Joining	*Percentage of Members*
1990–1993	26.0
1994–1999	27.0
2000	47.0
Total	100.0

households obtained membership in SHGs in 2000 and after was the introduction of Swa-Shakthi programme in new villages from 1999 onwards. Otherwise, most of the groups formed by Grama Vikas were old with almost 10 years of existence.

Little less than half the members held positions of president and secretary during 2000 to 2003. About 57 per cent of the members did not hold any leadership position during this period, although some of them might have occupied these leadership positions prior to the year 2000 (Table 16).

Table 16: Distribution (%) of Members by Leadership Positions Held During 2000 to 2003

Position Held	*Percentage of Members*
President	24.0
Secretary	19.0
Not held any position	57.0
Total	100.0

As SHG members, households were required to contribute fixed amount of savings to the group. The amount contributed by each member was Rs.40 per month in most of the groups. The accumulated amount of savings by each member in the SHG varied from Rs.780 to Rs.6,850. The members having less than Rs.1,500 of accumulated savings was nearly one-third, while those having accumulated savings of Rs.1,500 to 2,000 constituted 32 per cent. The proportion of members with accumulated savings of more than Rs.2,000 was 37 per cent (Table 17). The amount of savings depended on the period of stay in the group.

Table 17: Distribution (%) of Members by Total Amount of Accumulated Savings in the Group

Total Amount (Rs.) of Savings	*1990–93*	*1994–99*	*2000*	*Total*
< 1,000	0.00	0.00	100.00	2
1,000 – 1,500	6.90	13.79	79.31	29
1,500 – 2,000	15.63	34.38	50.00	32
2,000 – 3,000	42.11	31.58	26.32	19
3,000 – 4,000	53.85	38.46	7.69	13
4,000 above	80.00	20.00	0.00	5
Total	26.00	27.00	47.00	100

Sources of Credit

The member households had utilised multiple sources of credit during the period 2000–2003 (Table 18). All the members obtained loans from the bank through the NABARD programme on bank-SHG linkage at least once. The proportion of members obtaining credit facility from their SHG was only 40 per cent during the last three years. The dependence on moneylenders and relatives/ friends was somewhat heavy. Table 18 shows that 32 per cent of the members had obtained one or two loans from the moneylenders during the period 2000–03. In contrast, the proportion of members obtaining loans directly from the banks was only 5 per cent.

Table 18: Distribution of Members (%) by Number of Loans Obtained from Different Sources of Credit During 2000 to 2003

Source	*Zero*	*One*	*Two*	*Total*
NABARD through SHG	0.0	88.0	12.0	100.0
SHG	60.0	26.0	14.0	100.0
Moneylenders	68.0	28.0	4.0	100.0
Relatives/ Friends	84.0	16.0	0.0	100.0
Bank	95.0	5.0	0.0	100.0

Several combinations of sources of credit were tried out by the member households (Table 19). As can be expected, the most frequently tried out combinations were NABARD loan and loans from NABARD as well as SHG. The next important combination was NABARD, moneylenders and SHGs. Table 19 shows that 26 per cent of the households had tried out this combination. The combination of NABARD and relatives was also important for the sample households.

It needs to be noted that the average amount went up substantially in the case of combinations where moneylenders and relatives were present. For instance, the average loan amount was nearly Rs.20,000 in the case of those households which had borrowed from both NABARD and moneylenders. In the case of four households borrowing from NABARD, moneylenders and relatives, the average loan amount was as much as Rs.41,075. This shows that whenever households borrowed from moneylenders and relatives, they needed larger loan amounts. On the other hand, if households had borrowed only from NABARD or from both NABARD and SHG, the average loan amount tended to be low around Rs.4,346 to Rs.6,303.

Table 19: Distribution of Members by Sources of Credit

Sources of Loan	*No. of Members*	*Total Amount (Rs.)*	*Average Amount (Rs.)*
NABARD through SHG	32	201,700	6,303
NABARD + SHG	22	95,602	4,346
NABARD + Moneylenders	13	257,420	19,802
NABARD + SHG + Moneylenders	13	203,738	15,672
NABARD + Bank + Moneylenders	2	71,000	35,500
NABARD + Bank	1	6,000	6,000
NABARD + Bank + Relatives	1	18,000	18,000
NABARD + Moneylenders + Relatives	4	164,300	41,075
NABARD + Relative	7	119,600	17,086
NABARD + SHG + Bank	1	11,445	11,445
NABARD + SHG + Relatives	4	51,109	12,777
Total	100	1,199,914	11,999

The total picture on different sources of credit can be obtained from Table 20. During the last three years, 100 sample households obtained Rs.11.80 lakhs. Nearly 40 per cent of this amount was obtained from the banks under the linkage programme. Interestingly, the next important source was moneylenders who accounted for more than 37 per cent of the total loan amount. Relatives and friends accounted for nearly 16 per cent of the total amount. Why did the member households prefer moneylenders and relatives although interest rates in the case of former were very high? Table 20 provides the reasons for borrowing from moneylenders and relatives/ friends.

- The maximum loan that could be obtained from moneylenders and relatives was substantively higher than that from the bank and SHGs.
- The average loan amount from moneylenders and relatives was around Rs.12,000, while it was only Rs.4,195 in the case of banks and the linkage programme.
- Borrowing from the banks and NABARD meant delays. The average time taken to obtain a loan in the case of banks directly and under the linkage programme was 57 and 40

days, respectively. On the other hand, moneylenders and relatives provided the loan within a week.

- It was also expensive to borrow from the banks.
- Since the loan amounts from the banks were insufficient, member households preferred to borrow from moneylenders and relatives.
- The percentage of repayment was high in the case of NABARD and moneylenders as there had been continuous follow up.

After discussing the borrowings from different sources of credit, let us now concentrate only on credit obtained from the banks through SHGs. First, let us discuss the purpose-wise distribution of credit.

Purposes of Borrowing from the Banks

A distribution of households by purpose of loan utilisation that had been stated in the application form has been provided in Table 21. Most of the households stated that they would utilise the loan amount for agriculture, dairying and livestock rearing. While 29 per cent of the households stated that they would utilise the loan amount for crop production, 8 per cent stated the purpose as construction of new irrigation sources. As many as 33 and 18 per cent of the households borrowed from banks by stating that they would use the loan amount for dairying and livestock rearing, respectively. Thus, as far as the stated purpose was concerned, 91 per cent of the households mentioned in the application form that they would utilise the bank loans for productive activities.

The distribution of households by the purpose for which loan amount was actually utilised was different (Table 21) at least in respect of dairying and livestock. In the case of these two activities the fungibility was most evident. Some of the households borrowing for dairying and livestock rearing had actually used the loan amount for house construction, consumption and purchase of assets.

The difference between the stated and the actual purpose of loan utilisation has two implications. First, the proportion of households utilising the loan amount for productive purposes was less. Second, in the case of 15 per cent of the households, the loan amount borrowed from the banks did not result in tangible income, though such utilisation might have provided security and other forms

Table 20: Basic Details on Different Sources of Credit

Sources	*Loan Amount (in Rs.)*	*Loan Amount (%)*	*Minimum Amount of Loan (in Rs.)*	*Maximum Amount of Loan (in Rs.)*	*Average Time Taken to Obtain Loan (in Days)*	*Average Amount of Loan (in Rs.)*	*Average Expenses (in Rs.)*	*Interest Range (% Per Annum)*	*Total Amount Repaid (in Rs.)*	*Total Amount Repaid (%)*
NABARD	469,820	39.8	1,000	16,000	40	4,195	22	24	369,327	47.7
Moneylenders	441,500	37.4	500	50,000	7	11,932	14	24 to 60	287,125	37.1
Relatives/ Friends	186,500	15.8	500	50,000	6	12,433	8	0	87,500	11.3
SHG	44,294	3.8	60	7,000	7	820	12	24	27,004	3.5
Bank	37,800	3.2	3,000	15,000	57	7,560	145	12 to 24	2,900	0.4
Total	1,179,914	100.0							773,856	100.0

of benefits. Because of the latter, the discussion on the impact of NABARD loans on income and reinvestment had to be confined to only 85 households which had invested the loan amount for some or the other income generation activities.

Table 21: Distribution of Households (%) by Purpose for Which Loan was Obtained and Purpose for Which it Was Utilised

	Purpose of Loan	*Utilised*
Agriculture	29.0	29.0
Irrigation	8.0	8.0
Dairying	33.0	27.0
Livestock	18.0	17.0
Non-agricultural activity	3.0	4.0
House construction	7.0	9.0
Consumption and others	2.0	4.0
Purchase of assets	0.0	2.0
Total (numbers)	100	100

Income from Activities

A discussion on the impact of borrowing from the banks under the NABARD programme on income becomes important since the programme aims at poverty alleviation. It would be interesting to discuss such an impact by purposes for which the loan amount was actually utilised. Table 22 provides the distribution of households by income received from activities for which loan amount was utilised and purpose of the loan. It might be noted that gross income was taken into consideration here as it was difficult to arrive at net income. Secondly, in the case of livestock rearing activity, some of the households had purchased livestock assets and they were yet to sell these assets. In such cases, imputed income was taken into consideration.

Of the 100 households, 30 per cent obtained income in the range of Rs.5,000 to Rs.20,000. As many as one-fourth of the households had not received any income. If one took Rs.20,000 as the cut off point for enabling the households to cross the poverty line, Table 22 reveals that 81 per cent of the households had received less than Rs.20,000 income and hence, the poverty alleviation impact of the programme seemed to be less discernible. Did this differ across the purposes for which the loan amount was utilised?

Table 22: Income from the Activity Undertaken from NABARD Loan

Activity Undertaken	*Distribution of Households (%) by Income (Rs.) Received from the Activity Taken with NABARD Loan*							*Total (No.)*
	No Income	*<2,500*	*2,500 – 5,000*	*5,001 – 10,000*	*10,001 – 20,000*	*20,001 – 50,000*	*50,001 & above*	
Agriculture	24.14	27.59	6.90	3.45	24.14	6.90	6.90	29
Irrigation	37.50	0.00	0.00	12.50	12.50	25.00	12.50	8
Dairying	0.00	0.00	14.81	33.33	22.22	22.22	7.41	27
Livestock	0.00	23.53	47.06	29.41	0.00	0.00	0.00	17
Non-agricultural activity	0.00	0.00	0.00	0.00	0.00	25.00	75.00	4
House construction	100.00	0.00	0.00	0.00	0.00	0.00	0.00	9
Consumption and others	100.00	0.00	0.00	0.00	0.00	0.00	0.00	4
Purchase of assets	100.00	0.00	0.00	0.00	0.00	0.00	0.00	2
Total	25.00	12.00	14.00	16.00	14.00	11.00	8.00	100

As expected, there was no income in the case of 15 per cent of the households, which utilised the loan amount for house construction, consumption and purchase of assets such as house sites. Surprisingly, a large proportion of households borrowing for agriculture and irrigation also did not receive any income. In the case of those households utilising the bank loan for agriculture, only 14 per cent received income more than Rs.20,000. In general, the proportion of households receiving more than Rs.20,000 of income was high in the case of households using the loan amount for non-agricultural activities (barber shop, petty shop, etc.), irrigation and dairying in that order. This can be attributed to the following. The income from dairying was high in the case of those households which were located in the villages with marketing facility and those investing larger amounts on the activities. The ventures relating to irrigation were successful in those villages where the groundwater table was good. In the case of livestock rearing, agriculture and dairying, accounting for the maximum proportion of loans, the income was either non-existent or less than Rs.20,000. Why is it that the income received from the activities has been very low?

- The activities such as dairying and livestock rearing did not provide any significant income during 2000–03. This was because the households had acquired livestock belonging to tender age, and such assets did not provide any significant income. The households were still having the hope that there would be some income in the future.

- Some of the households received less income from livestock rearing as they sold assets since there was severe drought condition in the last three years.
- The households, which had invested on agriculture and irrigation, had also obtained lower income due to the drought.

It would be interesting to know the position on the total income of the households including that from the activities for which the bank loans were utilised. It also becomes important to find out whether those not receiving any income from the activities for which loans were obtained were better or worse off in general terms. Table 23 provides the distribution of households by total income in 2002–03. If one takes Rs.20,000 as the income of BPL households, it appears that 56 per cent of the households received less than Rs.20,000 and hence, could be considered as poor. A direct implication of this is that the borrowing from the banks under the linkage programme of NABARD did not have any significant impact on the total income of the households. In the case of others the total income was more than Rs.20,000. In the case of 12 per cent of the households the income was in the range of above Rs.50,000 and these households could be considered as better-off.

Table 23: Distribution of Household Income (2002–2003)

Activity Undertaken	*Distribution of Households (%) by Total Household Income (Rs.)*								*Total (No.)*
	5,000 – 10,000	*10,000 – 15,000*	*15,000 – 20,000*	*20,000 – 25,000*	*25,000 – 30,000*	*30,000 – 50,000*	*50,000 – 1 Lakh*	*1 Lakh Above*	
Agriculture	10.34	24.14	17.24	10.34	10.34	17.24	10.34	0.00	29
Irrigation	12.50	12.50	12.50	0.00	0.00	37.50	12.50	12.50	8
Dairying	14.81	7.41	25.93	11.11	11.11	25.93	0.00	3.70	27
Livestock	29.41	41.18	11.76	5.88	5.88	0.00	0.00	5.88	17
Non-agricultural activity	0.00	25.00	0.00	0.00	0.00	0.00	25.00	50.00	4
House construction	22.22	22.22	22.22	11.11	0.00	11.11	0.00	11.11	9
Consumption and others	50.00	25.00	0.00	0.00	0.00	0.00	0.00	25.00	4
Purchase of assets	0.00	50.00	0.00	0.00	50.00	0.00	0.00	0.00	2
Total	17.00	22.00	17.00	8.00	8.00	16.00	5.00	7.00	100

Table 23 shows that the activities for which the loan amount was taken did not have much impact on the overall income of the households. For instance, although nearly one-fourth of the households obtaining loans for crop production reported no income from the activity, the total income in their case was more than Rs.20,000 among 48 per cent of the households. This can also been seen in the case of those households borrowing for irrigation.

Table 24, which gives the proportion of income earned from activities for which bank loan was utilised to total income, provides an idea on the extent to which bank loans made a difference to member households. Interestingly, in the case of over half of the households, the proportion of income from the activities for which loan was taken to total income was zero. The impact of drought is reflected in the sense that from nearly 80 of the members who had taken loan for agriculture, the contribution was nil.

Table 24: Proportion of Income from the Activity to Total Income of the Household

Activity Undertaken	*Distribution of Households (%) by Proportion of Income from Activity to Total Household Income*				
	Zero	*< 25*	*25 – 50*	*50 – 75*	*75–100*
Agriculture	79.31	3.45	10.34	3.45	3.45
Irrigation	62.50	25.00	12.50	0.00	0.00
Dairying	18.52	29.63	33.33	11.11	7.41
Livestock	23.53	47.06	29.41	0.00	0.00
Non-agricultural activity	0.00	25.00	50.00	25.00	0.00
House construction	100.00	0.00	0.00	0.00	0.00
Consumption and others	100.00	0.00	0.00	0.00	0.00
Purchase of assets	100.00	0.00	0.00	0.00	0.00
Total	52.00	20.00	20.00	5.00	3.00

Apart from drought, other factors had also contributed to low income from the activities. In the ensuing chapter, an attempt has been made to explain the factors which have contributed to the low proportion of income from activities for which loan amounts were obtained to total income.

6

Factors Contributing to Low Income

Insufficient Loan Amounts

Insufficient loan amount was an important factor for less income received by the sample households. It may be recalled that the banks extend credit facility on the basis of 1:1 to 1:4 ratio of savings in the group to loan amount. Since half of the groups were formed in 1999 and 2000, the savings amount was low. This meant that the total loan amount received from the banks was low in the case of half of the groups.

Did the members find the loan amounts to be insufficient? An answer to this question was sought to be found out by comparing the amount spent on the activities to the total loan amount received. If the amount spent was less than the total amount borrowed, this was a situation of over-financing on the part of the banks. On the other hand, if the amount invested was more than the amount borrowed, this again referred to a situation of over-financing. Table 25 provides the distribution of households by the proportion of amount invested on the activity to the total loan amount and size classes of landholding. Only 19 per cent of the households spent exactly the same amount as was obtained from the banks. About 17 per cent of the households spent less than the loan amount obtained from the banks. In the case of as many as 64 per cent of the households, the amounts invested on activity were higher than 100 per cent. In the case of 30 per cent of the households the proportion was more than 150 per cent. Thus, the loan amounts obtained from the bank were insufficient in the case of 64 per cent of the households. In the case of 30 per cent of the households, the loan amounts were grossly insufficient.

There is inverse relationship between the size class of landholdings and the proportion of amount spent on activity to the bank loan. In general, the amount invested on the activity was either less than or equal to the loan amounts in the case of most of the landless and marginal farmers. On the other hand, the proportion of the amount spent for the bank loan was higher in the case of small, medium and large farmers.

Table 25: Proportion of the Amount Spent on Activity to the Bank Loan Obtained

Size Class of Land-holding (in Acres)	*Distribution of Households (%) by Proportion of Loan Amount Spent to the Bank Loan Sanctioned*					*Total (No.)*
	< 99	*100*	*100–150*	*150–200*	*200 Above*	
Landless	37.50	25.00	37.50	0.00	0.00	8
0–1	21.88	12.50	34.38	12.50	18.75	32
1–2.5	14.81	22.22	25.93	18.52	18.52	27
2.5–5	9.09	18.18	45.45	0.00	27.27	22
5–10	14.29	14.29	28.57	14.29	28.57	7
10 above	0.00	50.00	25.00	0.00	25.00	4
Total	17.00	19.00	34.00	10.00	20.00	100

In which activities the loan amounts were generally insufficient? In the case of livestock rearing and agriculture, the loan amounts sanctioned were equal or more than the amount that was actually spent on the activity. This suggests that over-financing characterised these two income generation activities. On the other hand, the loan amounts were generally insufficient in the case of house construction, irrigation and dairying (Table 26).

Table 26: Proportion of the Amount Spent on the Activity to the Bank Loan by Purpose

Purpose	*Distribution of Households (%) by Proportion of Loan Amount Spent to the Bank Loan Sanctioned*					*Total (No.)*
	< 99	*100*	*100–150*	*150–200*	*200 Above*	
Agriculture	6.67	33.33	33.33	16.67	10.00	30
Irrigation	0.00	0.00	62.50	0.00	37.50	8
Dairying	21.88	3.13	37.50	15.63	21.88	32
Livestock	44.44	22.22	33.33	0.00	0.00	18
Non-agricultural activity	0.00	66.67	0.00	0.00	33.33	3
House construction	0.00	14.29	0.00	0.00	85.71	7
Consumption and others	0.00	50.00	50.00	0.00	0.00	2
Total	17.00	19.00	34.00	10.00	20.00	100

The reasons for insufficient loan amounts were as follows: First, the banks gave loan amounts on the basis of accumulated savings. Second, a few of the SHGs resorted to the practice of giving loans to all the members on the basis of savings contributed by each member. Now the question is, when faced with a situation of insufficient loan amounts, how did the member households manage?

Managing Insufficient Loan Amounts

Across all the purposes, the total amount borrowed was Rs.403,100 while the amount spent was Rs.957,920 (Table 27). Thus, the total amount of deficit for all the activities was Rs.554,820. The deficit was high in the case of house construction, irrigation, dairying and non-agricultural activities.

Table 27: Amount (Rs.) Spent and Amount Borrowed for Different Purposes

Purpose	*Amount Borrowed*	*Amount Spent*	*Difference*	*Used for Different Purpose*
Agriculture	90,200	117,850	–27,650	1,500
Irrigation	56,500	206,000	–149,500	0
Dairying	169,800	263,350	–93,550	7,300
Livestock	48,000	46,720	1,280	3,450
Non-agricultural activity	9,000	46,000	–37,000	0
House construction	24,600	272,000	–247,400	0
Consumption and others	5,000	6,000	–1,000	0
Total	403,100	957,920	–554,820	12,250

How did the sample households manage the deficit? The households managed to bridge the gap between the loan amount sanctioned and the actual amount spent with the help of five different sources (Table 28).

- Own savings were important means to bridge the deficit especially in the case of house construction, dairying, agriculture and irrigation.
- Relatives provided Rs.147,200 to meet the deficit. They were particularly helpful in the case of house construction and irrigation.

- Moneylenders contributed Rs.127,500 towards meeting the deficit. They were important sources in meeting the deficit relating to non-agricultural activities, irrigation, dairying and house construction.
- The government provided subsidies for house construction and dairying.
- SHGs provided only Rs.4,000 to meet the deficit. Such a low contribution from SHGs was due to the fact that once a member household borrowed from the bank through the group, it was not eligible to borrow from the group again until the bank loan was repaid.

Table 28: Sources of Excess Amount Mobilised (in %)

Purpose	*SHG*	*Money-Lenders*	*Relative*	*Own Savings*	*Govern-ment*	*Total (in Rs.)*
Agriculture	0.00	15.44	13.72	70.84	0.00	29,150
Irrigation	0.00	35.12	36.79	28.09	0.00	149,500
Dairying	0.00	18.34	27.96	33.86	19.83	100,850
Livestock	0.00	0.00	0.00	100.00	0.00	2,170
Non-agricultural activity	0.00	94.59	0.00	5.41	0.00	37,000
House construction	1.62	6.87	24.25	57.15	10.11	247,400
Consumption and others	0.00	0.00	0.00	100.00	0.00	1,000
Total	0.71	22.48	25.96	42.92	7.94	567,070

Thus, relatives and moneylenders played an important role in meeting the deficit. Although member households stated that the loans from relatives were interest free, this might not be the case in all the instances. We, therefore, looked at cases where borrowing from moneylenders and relatives formed an important proportion to the total amount spent on the activity. As expected, they played a significant role in productive activities, namely, irrigation, dairying and agriculture. Since they had to repay the loans to the moneylenders at more than 24 per cent interest rate, this became a huge burden and resulted in disastrous consequences. This is borne out by the experience of Jayamma (Case 1).

Case 1: Distress Sale of Assets to Repay the NABARD Loan

Jayamma, belonging to washerman community, is a small farmer owning 3 acres of land in Beemanatha village. She obtained a loan of Rs.16,000 for the lining of open well. In all, the total expenditure was Rs.60,000 on well construction, and obtaining pumpset with electricity connection. She borrowed Rs.34,000 from moneylenders to complete the well construction.

The income from cultivation was more than what the respondent expected during 2000–02 largely on account of good rainfall and more water in the open well. She repaid the loan obtained from moneylenders with income from agriculture and dairying. However, drought condition in 2002–03 resulted in low income from agriculture and she found it difficult to repay the loan amount which became Rs.20,000 along with the interest component. Though she was regularly paying the interest amount, the amount that she had to pay was Rs.18,000 in the middle of 2000. As the group was compelling her to repay the loan, she sold bullocks and cart worth Rs.17,000 for only Rs.13,000 to clear off the debt. When asked why the household had to resort to distress sale despite that the income from dairying was substantial, the son of SHG member noted that "what could we do when the group was forcing us to repay?"

Interest Burden

The rate of interest on bank loan was burdensome for most of the households given that the loan amounts were insufficient, there were compulsions to borrow from moneylenders, and unfavourable weather conditions in the last three years. This resulted in low effective incomes from activities undertaken with the support from the banks. Because of pressure from the groups, some of the members had to sell assets in order to repay the loan (see Case 2).

Case 2: Sale of Assets to Repay the Loan

Muniyamma from Virupakshi village obtained Rs.4,000 of NABARD loan in May 2000 to buy two cows, which could also be used for ploughing the land. The total amount spent for the purchase of two cows was Rs.12,000. She mobilised the remaining amount through borrowing from relatives (Rs.4,000) and sale of sheep (Rs.4,000). The household invested a large amount on two cows with the hope that they could be used for the cultivation of 0.5 acre of their own land and hiring them out for others in the village.

The hopes were belied due to irregular rainfall in the region since 2000–01. There was hardly any income in the first year of purchase. The meagre income obtained in the second year was used for the maintenance of animals and payment of accumulated interest. In the third year, there was no rain at all in the area. Fearing that obtaining fodder was going to be difficult, they sold two cows for only Rs.6,500 although the expected price was Rs.10,000. The household attributed the loss in the enterprise to external factors (drought and the consequent shortage of fodder) and high interest on the loan.

Further, the rule that the loan amount had to be repaid within one year put pressure on the member households. Although three years of repayment period was provided by the banks, this was not sufficient given that some of the households had been leading very difficult life. As the Case of Mangamma shows when there was crisis within the household, there was none to help and the result was accumulation of interest. The high interest on loans had disastrous consequences on her (Case 3).

Case 3: Disastrous Consequences of High Interest Loan on the Poor

Mangamma is a resident of Beemanatha village, and belongs to Backward caste (Agasa). She lives with her parents and son in a small *pucca* house. She is landless and depends on wage labour for livelihood. Her parents are old and depend on her. Her son, aged about 12 years, is already working as a wage labourer in agriculture.

Mangamma was deserted by her husband, returned to her parents' house and began to live with them and her elder brother. She joined the SHG formed by Grama Vikas in 1992, and began to contribute savings. In 1997, she obtained a loan of Rs.7,000 from NABARD through SHG at an annual interest rate of 24 per cent. She added Rs. 500 from her savings and purchased a cow for Rs. 7,500. With milk collection centre present in the village, and good grass available, she was getting good income from the sale of milk. She repaid Rs. 1,500 of the loan from the income earned from the activity. Meanwhile, her brother became sick. She incurred considerable expenditure towards hospitalisation. During the period of her brother's illness, she could not take care of the cow. When her brother's health condition deteriorated, she was not able to meet the hospital expenses, hence, sold the cow for Rs. 7,000. Her brother, however, did not recover and died. She became the only earning member in the household to support her parents and the child. She could not attend the meetings of SHG for a long time. The interest amount on the loan of Rs. 7,000 accumulated to Rs. 10,000. Her main worry was that the burden of repayment of the loan would fall on her young son. She stated that "If anything happens to me the burden of loan repayment will fall on my child who is 12 years old". With the implementation of Jala Samvardhana Programme by Grama Vikas, she was able to obtain regular wage work and started repaying half the wage amount of Rs. 40 per day. She has till now repaid Rs. 6,100 including interest. Now she has still to repay Rs. 10,540. She noted that she could not send the child to the school, and spend for health and other subsistence needs of the household. The case of Mangamma shows that if the household with NABARD loan faced crisis, the interest component would have disastrous consequences on the livelihood and health and subsistence needs.

Table 29 shows the interest burden by different categories of farmers. Although the interest burden was between 10 and 20 per cent in the case of most of the borrowers, it was more than 20 per cent in the case of 29 per cent of the borrowers. Interestingly, the interest burden was more in the case of marginal farmers followed by medium farmers.

Table 29: Proportion of Expenditure and Interest Paid to Total Amount Borrowed by Landholding Classes

Size Class of Land-holding (in Acres)	*Less than 10%*	*10 to 20 %*	*20 to 30%*	*30 to 54.40%*	*Total*
Landless	37.50	62.50	0.00	0.00	8
0–1	15.63	40.63	28.13	15.63	32
1–2.5	22.22	59.26	11.11	7.41	27
2.5–5	4.55	59.09	22.73	13.64	22
5 above	36.36	45.45	9.09	9.09	11
Total	19.00	52.00	18.00	11.00	100

Table 30 shows that the interest burden was more in the case of loans taken for irrigation and livestock rearing.

Table 30: Proportion of Expenditure and Interest Paid to Total Amount Borrowed by Purpose

Purpose	*Less than 10%*	*10 to 20 %*	*20 to 30%*	*30 to 54.40%*	*Total*
Agriculture	16.67	43.33	30.00	10.00	30
Irrigation	12.50	37.50	25.00	25.00	8
Dairying	25.00	56.25	9.38	9.38	32
Livestock	22.22	55.56	5.56	16.67	18
Non-agricultural activity	0.00	100.00	0.00	0.00	3
House construction	14.29	57.14	28.57	0.00	7
Consumption and others	0.00	50.00	50.00	0.00	2
Total	19.00	52.00	18.00	11.00	100

Loan Repayment

The total amount repaid was Rs.327,632 towards the total borrowed amount of Rs.403,100 (Table 31). As can be expected, the income from coolie work accounted for about one-third of total repayment.

This was particularly so in the case of agriculture, house construction and dairying. Importantly, sale of assets and borrowing accounted for nearly 30 per cent of the total amount repaid. The extreme measures of sale of assets were resorted to in the case of agriculture, irrigation, dairying and livestock rearing. The activity for which loan was taken contributed only about 25 per cent of the repayment of loan amount. This was very significant in the case of non-agricultural activity, dairying and irrigation.

Table 31: Distribution of Loan Repayment (%) by Different Sources

Purpose	*From the Activity*	*Through Coolie Work*	*Sale of Assets*	*Borrowing*	*From Agriculture*	*Others*	*Total (in Rs.)*
Agriculture	19.43	38.27	21.64	12.87	1.39	6.39	86,091
Irrigation	20.31	10.24	26.40	18.28	17.26	7.51	49,240
Dairying	34.57	32.52	16.64	4.20	4.81	7.27	119,014
Livestock	14.41	59.41	23.54	0.00	1.92	0.72	41,632
Non-agricultural activity	94.43	5.57	0.00	0.00	0.00	0.00	8,972
House construction	0.00	48.08	8.28	0.00	38.11	5.52	18,106
Consumption and others	0.00	83.61	0.00	16.39	0.00	0.00	4,577
Total	25.13	34.94	19.15	7.88	7.06	5.84	327,632

7

Conclusions

This study on the 'Impact of Bank Interest Rates on SHG Members' was initiated with the objective of analysing effects and ramifications of interest rates on SHG members under the bank-SHG linkage programme started by the NABARD. The study was initiated by Grama Vikas, a NGO in Mulbagal taluk in Kolar district, which has been working with women belonging to depressed castes and economically vulnerable groups for the last two decades. This study was aimed at assisting the Grama Vikas in its advocacy work relating to interest rates on bank loans through NABARD's bank-SHG linkage programme.

By the early 1990s, several success stories relating to micro-finance in different parts of the World began to unfold. In the context of inability of the commercial banks to provide loans to a large number of small borrowers without adequate physical collateral, it was thought that the poor in the SHGs could be linked with commercial banks. This was expected to improve the access of credit to the rural poor and, in the process, achieve the targets fixed under the priority sector lending. Accordingly, NABARD initiated a programme in 1992 to link the SHGs formed by the NGOs and other organisations such as banks, for both poverty alleviation and to achieve cost-effectiveness in reaching a large number of small borrowers in the rural areas. Although the programme made considerable progress in quantitative terms, a few concerns are often raised. In the context of a steep decline in the interest rates on bank deposits and different types of loans, several NGOs have expressed concern about the high interest rates on SHG loans at 12.5 per cent, emphasising the need for its reduction. Further, since the poorer sections covered under the programme earned their livelihood in adverse socio-economic and weather conditions, high interest loans result in smaller income from the activities assisted under the programme. This, in turn, lead to inability to invest in the activity and to incur expenditure on health, education and other subsistence needs.

Grama Vikas in its interactions with the people has found that the members have been finding it difficult to obtain sufficient income to repay the loan with interest, reinvest into the activity and meet the social expenditure of the household. The organisation has also learnt that the member borrowers repaid the loans by curtailing the expenditure on food, clothing, education and health. Further, some of the members had been forced to repay the loans by selling the productive assets that they had acquired through NABARD loan and/ or through their own sources. In some other cases, the loan had to be repaid through borrowing from moneylenders at high interest rates. Grama Vikas is concerned that all these come in the way of achieving the objectives of asset building, income generation and poverty reduction.

This study, therefore, examined the effects and ramifications of bank interest rates on SHG members. The main objectives of the study were to:

1. arrive at transaction costs incurred by the banks and SHGs under the programme of NABARD on Bank-SHG linkage;
2. analyse the impact of interest on income from the activity, investment into the activity and meeting the expenditure incurred on subsistence needs; and
3. find out whether there was any justification for advocacy to reduce interest rates on bank loans through NABARD programme.

The data were collected from 100 member households belonging to 20 randomly selected groups with the help of a structured questionnaire. Information was also collected from all the 20 sample groups and banks covering these groups.

Grama Vikas has been implementing micro-finance programme for the last 15 years for women members. By 1998, it had organised 172 SHGs for 3,790 women in 112 villages. The organisation provides awareness and builds the capacity of members, and incentives for regular savings contribution. The efforts of the organisation resulted in a rapid growth of total savings in the project area. By 1999, all the members in the project area had contributed savings of Rs.52.73 lakhs.

A group member in the project area of Grama Vikas could take loans from the savings fund, *Mahila Okkuta* (Federation of SHGs) and banks through NABARD SHG-linkage programme. By providing three sources of credit, the organisation helped the members to avail credit for different credit needs that the members had.

The sample villages differed in terms of caste composition. In most of the villages, SC/STs and backward castes were dominant. Most of the villages were located 10 kms away from the taluk headquarters. The villages had only basic government facilities such as primary school, mini water supply and milk co-operative society. In most of the villages, people depended on rain fed agriculture and grew ragi, groundnut and paddy. The cultivation of commercial crops such as vegetables, horticultural crops was possible only under irrigation. Thus, the sample SHGs were found in villages dominated by SC/STs and backward caste households. This implies that the SHGs had been located in poorer villages. Agriculture depended on rainfall, and hence, crop production loans did not have favourable conditions. The marketing facilities for milk production made the loans for dairying viable.

Since 1994, Grama Vikas has been collaborating with NABARD in the linkage programme. It has enabled the group members to avail loans from 15 commercial banks and RRBs in the last 10 years. The total number of loans obtained was 2,736 and the total amount of credit was 1.21 crores during the period 1994–2003. However, the average loan amount from the banks declined over a period. In the initial phases, dairying and livestock were the important activities for which the credit was provided. In the early 2000s, agriculture and non-agricultural activities also became important.

Transaction Costs to Banks

Information collected from seven bank branches shows that the number of SHGs assisted by the banks was disproportionately small in comparison to the number of villages in the service area. The total amount of outstanding loan to SHGs as a proportion of the total outstanding loan in the bank branch was negligible in the case of all the sample bank branches. This suggests that there is scope to increase the number of SHGs under the linkage programme.

Because of lower proportion of loans to SHGs in the overall

loan portfolio of bank branches, it is difficult to arrive at transaction costs separately for the linkage programme. Further, banks also do not maintain this information. Hence, the data on number of visits to SHGs, training, paper work and supervision have been analysed to obtain the broad picture on transaction costs. An analysis of these data show the following.

- In most of the cases, the bank officials did not visit the sample SHG or the number of visits was generally one or two. Hence, the transaction cost on account of visits to SHGs was not substantial to the bank branches.
- The bank managers stated that they did not provide any training to SHG members as it was generally perceived that the responsibility of providing training was vested with the NGO. Thus, the banks did not spend any money on training to SHG members.
- All the bank managers noted that the bank-SHG linkage programme had largely contributed to reduction in paper work. The costs on paper work in the case of bank-SHG linkage programme were minimum and considerably lower as compared to the other lending programmes such as crop loans, agricultural gold loans and term loans.
- A majority of the bank managers had perceived that there was significant reduction in the supervision costs under the bank-SHG linkage programme.
- Although bankers did not incur any significant costs towards training, selection and monitoring of the borrowers, the recovery rates under the linkage programme were significantly higher as compared to other programmes.

In conclusion, it can be stated that the sample banks were faced with win-win situation in so far as the linkage programme was concerned. They provided loans to a large number of the poor in the service area with minimum costs towards selection and supervision. In the process, they were able to save time and human resources, on the one hand, and to obtain good recovery rates and profitability in the whole operation, on the other.

Costs Incurred by SHGs

In contrast, costs incurred by the SHGs before, during and after obtaining loan from the banks were substantial on account of the following.

- SHGs ran around banks for one to four months due to a number of reasons which included lack of awareness on the linkage programme, repeated visits on account of non-availability of bankers, needed to comply with bank procedures. The costs on transportation were, therefore, substantial.
- It was often the case that more than two SHG members had to visit the bank not only to put pressure but also the requirement of the bankers that all members should be present when loan amount was disbursed. This meant that a larger number of members had to visit the bank and hence, the costs on transportation also went up.
- The distinct location of the banks also contributed to an increase in the transportation costs.
- The wage income foregone on account of repeated visits to the banks distantly located was substantially higher in the case of most of the sample SHGs.
- The SHGs had to incur expenditure on complying with bank procedures such as agreement on a bond paper. This resulted in considerable expenditure on paper work.
- The expenses in connection with the visits of bankers were either nil or not very high in most of the sample SHGs.
- It was the SHG which spent considerable time in the selection, monitoring and repayment of loans. During the period of borrowing and repayment of loans to the banks, the SHGs spent most of the time in group meetings for the management of bank loans. However, these costs could not be included as repayment was still going on in the case of most of the groups at the time of survey and it was difficult to work out imputed costs on time spent in the management of loans from the banks under the linkage programme.
- The SHGs also incurred loss on account of defaults. Although a couple of members from each group defaulted, the repayment to the bank was regular. This became possible due to regular savings contribution by all the members. The SHGs repaid to the banks notwithstanding a couple of

defaulters as they had been hoping to get the second loan from the bank. Nevertheless, costs on account of default were not included as most of the groups were still repaying and all the SHGs were confident that they would ultimately recover the loan amount from the defaulters.

In the case of six groups which had fully repaid the loan amount to the bank, the total costs including interest was between 14 and 44 per cent of the total loan amount obtained from the banks. This meant that the SHG members spent as much as Rs.14 to Rs.44 for every Rs.100 that they had borrowed from the bank. The costs were, therefore, steeply high for the SHG members, a majority of whom belonged to low income and depressed caste categories.

Impact of Interest on Income and Reinvestment

The information collected from 100 member households show that they depended on multiple sources of credit during the period 2000–03. All the members obtained loans from the bank through NABARD at least once. The dependence on moneylenders and relatives was somewhat heavy as the loan amount tended to be high in these cases and average time taken to obtain loan was relatively low.

Although 91 per cent of the members had given an undertaking to the banks that they would utilise the loan amount for productive purposes, the proportion of households utilising the loan amount for productive activities was only 85 per cent. The fungibility was high in the case of dairying.

The income from activities for which loan was obtained tended to be nil in the case of agriculture and irrigation due to continuous drought for three years. The income from the activity to the total household income was substantial only in the case of non-agricultural activities, ventures relating to irrigation and dairying as these activities provided regular income. The marketing facilities in the form of milk collection centres resulted in regular income in the case of households undertaking dairying and hence, this activity contributed significantly to the total household income.

However, the borrowing from banks under the linkage programme did not help nearly 50 per cent of the households to cross the poverty line. The reasons for low income from the activities were as follows. First, livestock assets were obtained at tender age, and the fattening of livestock animals was still going on. Second, faced with the situation of inability to find fodder on account of drought, some of the households had sold the livestock assets. Third, the household investing on agriculture and irrigation did not get high income on account of drought.

The incomes were also low on account of under-financing. The bank loans were found to be insufficient in the case of about two-thirds of sample households to undertake the income generating activities and for investing on assets. When faced with the situation of under-financing many households depended on moneylenders and relatives, and borrowed at exorbitant interest rates. The interest burden was, therefore, high. With recurring drought and adverse village conditions (such as decline in groundwater table, lack of fodder, etc), many households found it difficult to retain the assets. The repayment to the bank and moneylenders was made through sale of assets and coolie work rather than the activity for which the loan amount was obtained.

Most of the households perceived that 24 per cent interest rate on loans obtained from banks (12.5% to bank and 11.5% to SHG) was very high and felt that the bank should reduce the interest rate. When asked whether the SHG should also reduce the interest rate, most of them noted that SHGs should not reduce the interest rate as costs to them under the linkage banking programme was very high. Further, SHGs also undertook considerable work relating to the selection, monitoring and repayment of loans under the linkage programme. In other words, the SHG members perceived that banks were faced with win-win situation while SHGs and members were faced with loss-loss situation. The study also finds overwhelming evidence in support of the perceptions of SHG members.

The study, therefore, comes to the conclusion that there is a case for Grama Vikas, other NGOs, donors and development workers to advocate a reduction in the interest rates charged by the banks under the NABARD bank-SHG linkage programme, the primary objective of which is poverty alleviation.

Bibliography

Dasgupta, Rajaram (2001). An Informal Journey Through Self-Help Groups. *Indian Journal of Agricultural Economics*, 56(3): 370–86.

Goetz, Anne Marie and Rina Sen Gupta (1996). Who Takes the Credit? Gender, Power and Control Over Loan Use in Rural Credit Programs in Bangladesh. *World Development*, 24(1).

Harper, Malcolm (2002). *Promotion of Self-Help Groups under the SHG-Bank Linkage Programme in India*. Bombay: NABARD.

Hashemi, Syed M, Sidney Ruth Schuler and Ann P Riley (1996). Rural Credit Programs and Women's Empowerment in Bangladesh. *World Development*, 24(4).

Hulme, David (2000). Impact Assessment Methodologies for Micro-Finance: Theory, Experience and Better Practice. *World Development*, 28(1): 79–98.

Hulme, David and Paul Mosley (1996). *Finance Against Poverty*. London: Routledge.

Kropp, Erhard W and B S Suran (2002). *Linking Banks and Self-Help Groups in India: An Assessment*. Bombay: NABARD.

Mayoux, Linda (1998). Women's Empowerment and Micro-Finance Programs: Approaches, Evidence and Ways Forward. *Discussion Paper*. Milton Keynes: The Open University.

Morduch, Jonathan (1999). The Micro-Finance Promise. *Journal of Economic Literature*, XXXVII.

NABARD (1999). *Potential Linked Credit Plan: Kolar District*. Bangalore: NABARD.

Namboodiri, N V and R L Shiyani (2001). Potential Role of Self-Help Groups in Rural Financial Deepening. *Indian Journal of Agricultural Economics*, 56 (3): 401–9.

Puhazhendhi, V (1995). *Transaction Costs of Lending to the Rural Poor: Non-Governmental Organisations and Self-Help Groups of the Poor as Intermediaries for Banks in India*. Brisbane, Australia: Foundation for Development Co-operation.

Puhazhendi, V and K C Badatya (2002). *Self-Help Group Bank Linkage Programme for Rural Poor in India: An Impact Assessment.* Bombay: NABARD.

Rajasekhar, D (1993). Linking Two Worlds! Will Links between Formal Banks and Voluntary Credit Groups Work? *Dialogue,* 2(1).

Rajasekhar, D (2002a). Economic Programmes and Poverty Reduction: NGO Experiences from Tamil Nadu. *Economic and Political Weekly*, XXXVII (29): 3063–68.

Rajasekhar, D (2002b). Impact of Micro-Finance Programmes on Poverty and Gender Equality: Some Evidence from Indian NGOs. In Shahra Razavi (ed.), *Shifting Burdens: Gender and Agrarian Change under Neoliberalism*. Bloomfield, USA: Kumarian Press, Inc.

Rajasekhar, D (2004a). Micro-Finance and Poverty Alleviation Issues Relating to NGO Programmes in South India, *ISEC Working Paper Series, Working Paper No.146*, Bangalore: Institute for Social and Economic Change.

Rajasekhar, D (2004b). Micro-Finance, Poverty Alleviation and Empowerment of Women: A Study of Two NGOs from Andhra Pradesh and Karnataka, *ISEC Monograph No. 4*. Bangalore: Institute for Social and Economic Change.

Rogaly, Ben (1996). Micro-Finance Evangelism, Destitute Women and the Hard Selling of New Anti-Poverty Formula. *Development in Practice*, 6 (2).

Satish, P (2001). Some Issues in the Formation of Self-Help Groups. *Indian Journal of Agricultural Economics*, 56(3): 410–18.

Stiglitz, J E (1990). Peer Monitoring and Credit Markets, *The World Bank Economic Review*, 4(3): 351–67.

Index